Intercepted Planets: Possibilities for a New Age

Rev. Alice Miller

ISBN-10: 0-86690-610-X
ISBN-13: 978-0-86690-610-4

Cover Design: Jack Cipolla

Published by:
American Federation of Astrologers, Inc.
6535 S. Rural Road
Tempe, AZ 85283

www.astrologers.com

Printed in the United States of America

Dedicated to all those who march to a different drum
and to my beloved Guru Garth
You are the exceptional people destined to bring in the next age.

Books by Rev. Alice Miller

Principles of Astrology: Planets, Signs & Houses
Dynamics of Astrology: Interpreting Aspects
The Soul of Astrology: Inner Dimensions of the Modern Moon
The "Limits" of Astrology: Saturn for Today
Retrograde Planets and Consciousness
Nodes of the Moon
The Part of Fortune and the Astral Body
Designs for a New Age: The Grand Cross, Mystic and Other Rectangles*
Interceptions: Heralds of a New Age
Intercepted Planets: Possibilities for a New Age

A Coven of Planets: A Pagan Astrology
A Kabbalistic Design of Planets: Astrology's Tree of Life
Healing the Inner Child: The Astrology of Family Dysfunction
Getting Birth Charts on Target: Techniques Old and New

About this Book

This is the long anticipated second volume of the Interception Series. It addresses the way that interpretations of planets, the nodes, and Fortuna change when they fall within intercepted signs. Rev. Miller's interception work breaks new ground in the field of natal chart interpretation. It is written especially for those astrological students and professionals who have inhabited interceptions in their charts. As always, the underlying theme is Self Awareness.

About the Author

Alice Miller has been a practicing professional astrologer in the Denver area since 1983. Healing the human condition through astrology is her commitment and calling. Along with a catalog of books and professional services, she offers instructive articles and a Q&A service on her website www.lifeprintastrology.com. You are also invited to sign up for her free newsletter, by contacting her at astrominister1@yahoo.com.

A natural psychologist from birth, Rev. Miller loves people. Her background includes three years study in Science of Mind and thirty years in the service professions. She is a mother, foster mother, godmother, grandmother and great-grandmother. Much of her writing is gleaned from the laboratory of her own life. Experience is interwoven with intuition, for a deeply insightful look at how our natal environment affects our adult lives.

The author deeply appreciates all comments from readers. Address them to: astrominister1@yahoo.com or Rev. Alice Miller, 17190 Mt. Vernon Rd, Lot 65, Golden, CO 80401-3828.

Contents

Order of Chapters

In selecting the order of the chapters, I chose to pair the planets
according to the polarities of the signs they rule. Consequently, Uranus, ruler of Aquarius,
follows the Sun, ruler of Leo. This was done to reinforce
the importance of polarity in charts, and especially in the intercepted areas.
Since Venus rules two signs, Taurus and Libra, the Venus chapter is placed between Mars,
ruler of Aries and Pluto, ruler of Scorpio.

Foreword

From my earliest years, I was treated very differently from my four younger siblings. I was the constant target of my mother's criticism. Although I never did anything right, she loaded a great deal of the housework on me. It was the first inconsistency I noticed, realizing that if my work was as inferior as she claimed, she would not have kept me doing it. Rather than let her destroy my self-image, I simply concluded that she did not mean it. Later, I realized that she simply lied. To cover up her own depression and lack of motivation, she convinced my father that I was lazy and useless, and should be punished for it. In the end, I grew up in spite of my parents, not because of them.

Still, being what I am, I could never hate them. I understood quite early in life that my mother was seriously handicapped—emotionally or morally. She did not seem to know how to love. I also noticed that my father was quite different out in the fields, away from her, than he was at home. I understood that he loved me, but was unwilling or unable to resist her control. A great joy of my life occurred many years later when he asked my forgiveness for the beatings she instigated and he administered.

These details are given to illustrate the fact that, from its beginning, my life was a far departure from normal. The saving grace of my childhood was that, while somewhat socially handicapped, I had far less emotional scarring than my sisters—who were actually treated much better than I. I came to realize that I had been born with some strength and/or wisdom that allowed me to overcome a great deal of soul-wounding with minimal scarring. In time, I came to realize that it came out of my interception, and especially my intercepted Aries Sun. But that was years later.

Meanwhile, I married at age seventeen and at twenty-five was the mother of four children. As I neared age thirty, the first marriage ended to be replaced several years later by a second. By that time my health was reaching a crisis point. I suffered from multiple infections and chronic depression.

Approaching my fortieth year, with my health severely damaged, a second marriage was coming apart at the seams, and we were in danger of losing the home that our family had built. Then it was that a higher power stepped in. I was diagnosed with hypo-glycemia and put myself on a proper diet, which began returning my energy to me. Soon after, I was introduced to some excellent nutritional supplements and created my own design for improved health. Feeling healthy for the first time in years, I got out more. Soon friends introduced me to metaphysics and astrology. By the time my last child graduated from high school and left home in my forty-third year, I was completely rejuvenated and ready to begin my real life.

From that time on, although periodic financial crises threatened, they were always managed. Two more ventures into marriage proved disastrous, but were short-lived. I survived and continued to learn and grow as an astrologer-metaphysician. It has been an incredible journey! Although to date it has not made me financially wealthy, my life is filled with riches. I do work that I love and meet wonderful people who share my view of the world, and all without leaving my office. The Internet, which was not even an idea in my childhood, has become my perfect environment. Today, my outreach is worldwide even though, as this is written, I have never traveled far enough from the center of the United States to see an ocean. How great is that!!

Rev. Alice Miller

Background:
The Rise in Human Consciousness

Part I: Planetary Symbols

From my vantage point in the early years of the twenty-first century, I will review the approach to the Age of Aquarius. It is clear to me that a new age represents a new phase of human development, but human development does not, cannot, happen overnight. The process is gradual and takes several centuries. The current shift is symbolized by the discovery of the planet Uranus in 1781. Linked to the industrial revolution, the most significant development that emerged was the gradual increase in free time that allowed humankind to think beyond the range of simple survival. Education became possible for the masses. Human minds were *off and running*.

Neptune's discovery in 1846 is generally linked to the birth of spiritualism. Small groups of people on the fringes of society began the process of legitimizing mediumship. A new church developed, nominally Christian, but largely ostracized by Christianity. Still, psychic research was being conducted and the synthesis of Eastern and Western belief systems had begun.

Pluto entered the scene in 1930. The planet is symbolically linked to the development of psychology and particle physics. The human subconscious became the scapegoat for all human consciousness that fell outside the socially acceptable range. Meanwhile, another branch of science was developing skills with the potential to destroy the world. Initially, one threatened our sanity and the other our lives. Still, the recognition of the creative aspects of human consciousness is rooted in this period.

Finally, in 1977, came the discovery of Chiron. Interestingly enough, it is not at the outer fringes of the solar system. Instead, it has an eccentric orbit that crosses the paths of both Saturn and Jupiter, beginning a bit beyond Mars and moving nearly into Uranus' path. Still controversial, even its classification is in question. Is it a planet or an asteroid? Some have settled on a new term, *planetoid*.

By whatever name, I believe it to be the new ruler of Virgo. Even now, in my practice, I can see Virgo clients emerging from the old Mercury rulership to the more expanded abilities conferred by Chiron. Clearly, this planet is the symbolic ruler of the information age—the mechanical correlation to the raising of human consciousness. At the least, the World Wide Web is a convenient way to explain why today's children are so much more aware than their parents.

Part II: Neptune's Role in the Expansion of Consciousness

Throughout recorded history, there has not been a time when some part of humanity did not see, hear, or sense angels, fairies, elves, discarnate spirits, and/or alien beings. Just outside the *normal* range of human senses, help for humanity was always present, although the form it took varied according to the belief systems of the times.

Very young children often saw and spoke with these beings. When they mentioned doing so, a common adult response was to chuckle over the child's imagination. Adult laughter caused most children to give up their ability to see what adults could not. Those few born with much wider perceptual ranges often continued to see, hear or sense these beings, but learned not to speak of them.

A less common and more harmful response was fear-born condemnation. Those who could not stop such *unacceptable* sensory experiences were often made to believe that what they were seeing was demonic and the seers spiritually contaminated. So it was that it was only socially acceptable to see *pink elephants* when one was intoxicated. How much alcoholism develops as a cover for extrasensory experience? How many people chose slow suicide over being labeled evil or insane? And, in more recent times, how many hallucinogenic *trips* made cover stories for those whose sensory abilities included seeing or hearing that which was beyond the ordinary range of human senses?

Neptune symbolizes our intuitive/psychic abilities. Dissolving boundaries—especially the boundaries on human perception—Neptune allows us to see, hear, or sense in ways not available to ordinary Mercury perception.

Beginning in the 1930s, when Neptune moved into Virgo, the general population began to be born with a visibly evolving consciousness structure. The vast majority of that first fourteen-year generation "lost" its expanded abilities early in life, but a few retained them. Then, every fourteen years, as Neptune moved across Libra, Scorpio, Sagittarius, Capricorn and now Aquarius, the human perceptual band continued to widen. By the last quarter of the century, sightings of, and information from, trans-human beings could no longer be completely ignored. Even many older people began to resurrect abilities previously traded for the approval of parents, teachers and religious leaders.

Today, television and movies show us what we are all becoming aware of in a way that the general population can accept without violation of their programming. As a result, the taboos against the various elements of extra sensory perception are fading fast. We are preparing for a new age, with a new definition of humanity. That definition will include the new abilities now gaining acceptance—the acceptance that allows them to grow into more adept and practical forms. We predict that by the end of the twenty-first century the *weird people* will be those who deny these abilities.

Part III: The Role of Interceptions in the Development of Consciousness

My research shows that those with intercepted areas in their natal horoscopes are those beings who were *born outside the general consciousness*. The inclusion of planets within interceptions increases the *distance* beyond the recognized *norm* or *average*. In essence, it may be said that such individuals are born with a consciousness level characteristic of the approaching age—or sometimes, the previous one—rather than the current one.

If we think of human consciousness as having a range from one to ten, we may say that the general population currently ranges from three to seven. People with interceptions in their natal horoscopes have a consciousness range above seven—the Possibility People—or below three—Regressives. Positive interceptions mark the groups that are leading the way to the next age, by demonstrating new ways of being and doing. Their lives *look different* from the social norm because they are on Earth to develop new ways of doing and being. And because they are, they often attract high levels of resistance from those around them.

Negative interceptions mark those who wish to return to the past and/or stop progress into the future. Using the chart alone, there is no certain method to determine whether an interception is positive or negative. Usually, one can only judge by the effects on the lives of others. Probably those charts with the rulers of the intercepted signs also intercepted should be scrutinized especially carefully because they would require much more effort to become sufficiently conscious for positive use. This would emphasize positive or negative qualities.

While we recognize the existence of certain regressed interceptions, in this book I give them little emphasis because they are generally satisfied with their current state. Rarely, if ever, does one of these people come for a chart reading. However, because they are often found as parents, siblings or mates of those with progressed interceptions, we need to acknowledge their existence.

They are found there because of the principle "Like attracts Like." The *likeness* in the attraction is that both are *outside the general consciousness*. Also, positive or negative, such individuals have more personal power than others, simply because of the intensity involved. Their potential for creativity or destructiveness is far greater than the norm.

How that power is used is the best criterion for judging these charts/lives. Possibility People are consciously creating their lives. Regressives use the same power for control of others. Advanced beings have little ability to detect evil because they contain none. Consequently, they cannot see the intent of those who would fasten themselves to their lives with the intent of using them for their own ends.

Tough love is the first lesson for most positively intercepted natives. Only when the true Possibility People—a correct term for those with positive interceptions—are free of these human parasites can they fully realize and develop whom and what they are.[1]

Part IV: The Possibility People

While such individuals have always existed, it is my belief that they increase markedly as each new age approaches. It is apparent to many that there was a major influx of advanced beings—with wider perceptual bands—beginning in the 1930s and 1940s. To symbolize the process now in motion, we may say that the average range of human consciousness is moving upward from the three-to-seven bracket into the range of four to eight—the norm for the next age.

There are six possible interceptions, composed of the six sign polarities. The occasional chart has more than one interception. More commonly, the meaning of the interception is expanded through the inclusion of planets within it.

Each intercepted polarity has its own characteristics and general designation. For full descriptions of these, see my book, *Interceptions: Heralds of a New Age*. Here you will find a method for delineating interceptions. You will also find a description of the types of family dysfunction experienced—if only due to the fact of there being no adequate parenting available for such advanced beings. And, most important, you will find the ultimate metaphysical meaning and purpose of each interception. It is highly recommended that my interception books be regarded as a set and used together.

The great lesson in being a Possibility Person is that, born outside the general consciousness, we must learn to live there. This means that we must develop our creativity, learning to use affirmations, visualizations and/or rituals in place of, or to supplement, ordinary methods for mundane activities like finding jobs, making major purchases (cars, homes, etc.), selecting friends, lovers and/or mates, and creating money. We are

---

[1]In the past we have used terms borrowed from others. Some of these are Starseed, Pleadians, Lightbearers, etc. These terms generally refer to advanced beings, many of whom would have intercepted charts. However, the clearest definition for natives with positive interceptions is Possibility People.

developing new methods of relating and of providing protection and security for ourselves and our children. As we do so, we become *living lessons*, teaching others by example. In this way we seed and midwife the next age. Exceptions to the general population now, we are what humanity is intended to become.

Possibilities and the Rise in Human Consciousness

Committed relationships are a major issue. Today the accepted social model is based on the idea of two halves making a whole and mutual or co-dependency. *Chemistry* has replaced common sense in the choosing of significant others. The result looks like a disaster for adults and children alike. Surely it is time to revise our ideas about the purpose, meaning, and structure of commitment. It is time to question the usefulness of this model. It is also time to consider these questions: Could it be that humans evolve to a level of wholeness that precludes the need for this *other half*? Do they become competent to parent alone? Are the children sufficiently advanced to require less parenting?

Financial issues are especially important in that so many of us have been conditioned to the idea that there is something spiritual about poverty. There is not, and that is a major issue for the general consciousness. The Piscean age put great emphasis on *suffering saints*, *yogi masters with begging bowls*, and *crucified Christs.* During most of that age the great lesson was that we are the children of Divinity. Our relationship with Source was that of little children to a Divine Parent.

As the Age of Aquarius approaches, we can realize the full extent of our Divine Genetics. We are both the legal and genetic heirs to Original Being. As such, over lifetimes, we are meant to grow up to be like that One. The general population has been developing its inner senses over the last century or so, with a dramatic increase in the final quarter of the twentieth century. Now the creative side of consciousness is rapidly emerging into visibility.

In the United States, metaphysical (Christian) churches are teaching *scientific prayer.*[1] In recent years there has also been a major Pagan Revival, including the teaching of divinitory techniques and ritual magic. By whatever name it is called, these are means of tapping into the creative side of consciousness. They all work and are meant to be used to an increasing degree as we move toward and into the next age.[2] They are all means for integrating our inheritance as creators-of-reality into our conscious thinking. I recommend that readers investigate one or more of these opportunities for learning greater control of their innate creative power.

---

[1]Notably the Church of Religious Science, Unity, and Divine Science.

[2]By our calculations the shift into the next age may occur around 2080. There is, however, no known way of calculating this exactly. Our method was to investigate future transits for a time when the energies fit our idea of what that should look like. We do not expect general agreement. It is, after all, merely a guess.

It is, however, equally important to be self-aware, to be familiar with our personal conditioning and its effects. Some may wish to *re-record* the *old tapes* in the subconscious. Others may find ways to make the existing conditioning more productive.[1] In the end, it does not matter so much what we do with/about our conditioning, as it does that we become aware of it. The advice generally ascribed to Socrates, to "Know Thyself" is still valuable. Using astrology for just that purpose is the major theme of all my writing, and every client reading that I do.

The Psychological Impact of Interceptions

Every interception of a sign or a planet indicates a *social handicap*—something comparable to a physical disability. By this I mean that it functions in some way different from the socially acceptable *norm*. We will not be able to use it in the generally accepted way, largely because it is of an evolutionary level different from that of the general population. Possibility People are more advanced than the general population, and especially so in the intercepted area of the chart. To get an idea of the effect of this, consider a visitor to our planet—one who looks like us—from a home world that had developed telepathy to an extent precluding spoken language. How well could she or he communicate with natives of Philadelphia, Denver, or San Francisco? The problem would arise—not from something *wrong* with our visitor—but from a higher evolutionary state. It might be necessary for our visitor to *remember* spoken language, before she or he could teach others to use their own telepathic gifts. She or he would be *socially handicapped,* and would never really *fit in* with the general population.

It is important to notice that with every physical disability comes the corresponding development of some other sense or ability. Those with poor hearing develop better vision, and the reverse. The blind develop their sense of touch and learn to read braille. Today, even those who cannot speak can learn to use a computerized device to speak for them. And so on.........

When natal horoscopes reveal such *limitations* as interceptions, we find that a full assessment of the chart will reveal a trend toward developing other abilities. What is initially a compensation can end as expanded awareness. Most obviously, the tendency to be somewhat socially handicapped focuses intercepted natives inwardly where new tools are developed for the tasks ahead. Then it is that both the individuals and those whose lives they touch discover greater possibilities of human function. Each of us increases awareness for self first, then for others. And that, above all, is the intent behind positive interceptions.

---

[1]This is the particular expertise of the author as a reader of natal horoscopes.

What Are Intercepted Planets?

Intercepted signs are enclosed entirely within their two houses. They do not appear on the cusp of any house. Because of this the chart will also have two pairs of matching house cusps. The tools for *opening* the interception are often contained in that area.

Intercepted planets—including the Nodal Axis and Fortuna—are caught within the interception, placed in the intercepted signs. Example: A client has Aries-Libra intercepted. Since his Sun and Mercury are in Aries and his Mars and Moon are in Libra, all four planets are intercepted.

How They Work Psychologically

The first great lesson of interceptions is that houses should be read as polarities. When any sign is intercepted, its polar opposite is also intercepted. Thus, when there is an interception in the first house, there must also be one in the seventh house.

Example: this interception (first-seventh) will represent an image problem and include a *partner* problem. Because the self-image is not well established, or not accurate—because it excludes the intercepted area from consciousness—it is impossible to know who our equals are. Consequently, we may marry those not our equals and the marriage (or other partnership) will not work well, largely because only one partner tries to make it work. Usually the underlying assumption—from the parental relationship—is that marriage/partnerships are not meant to be equal. There is a basic misconception that defines partnership as a co-dependant relationship: two people who *need* each other, or one who *needs* and one who *needs to be needed*, but who may or may-not love, or even like, each other.

When reading these charts, always begin with the intercepted signs and their location in the houses. In these houses, our early instructions are "*like the cusp sign*" and perhaps the sign after the interception, but "*not-like the intercepted sign.*" Planets inside the cusp signs add information. Those within the interception are excepted from the house of their placement—and to a certain extent from the entire chart. Their house message may be read, "without these planets." (See appendix I.)

At this level, planets generally follow the rules of logic. Consequently, a planet intercepted in, for example, the second house, will initially appear to function from the eighth. Either placement . . . in the eighth without interception or intercepted in the second . . . shows an instruction, either verbal or subliminal, to regard that planetary function as *not-good*, taboo, of no value to the child. It may/must be reclaimed later by the adult she or he becomes.

As an example, consider Mars intercepted in the second. Here desire is considered not-good. It does no good to want anything because you will not get it. (*Good children do not ask for anything.*) Natives often learn how to *need* the things that they want so that they can get them. Sometimes, very smart children learn to keep still about what they want, or occasionally pretend they do not want it, because that is the best way to get it.

Like the intercepted signs, intercepted planets represent a *social handicap*—as in the first example (first-seventh) above, which damages the ability to create a *successful marriage* according to the socially acceptable model. The inequality in relationship might be shown by an intercepted Saturn, which would *dump* all the responsibility within the relationship on one partner. (First house: It is not my responsibility. Seventh house: It is not your responsibility.)

In some way, intercepted areas either do not function, or function in a way different from the accepted norm. In the example above, the one who has the responsibility, may not have the right/the authority to make the changes necessary to transform dysfunction into function.

As with the signs, the underlying psychological cause of problems with intercepted planets is one or more assumptions,[1] made by the people who dominated our formative years.[2] This leaves most intercepted natives feeling somewhat uncomfortable in the existing environment. It feels like something is missing, that something has been left out of their makeup.

It is important to realize that nothing is left out of *you*. The wheel of houses describes the *environmental* factors of a birth chart. It is calculated from the time of day and loca-

---

[1] See *Interceptions: Heralds of a New Age.*
[2] The formative years are from before birth to approximately age seven, with the greater emphasis on the period before language is fully developed. Every birth chart reveals a great deal about this period because it is the foundation on which our lives are constructed.

tion of the birth. Thus, from the psychological perspective, the interception may be considered an overlooked or ignored area in that conditioning. The interception, then, represents something left out of, or incorrectly inserted into, your *education for life*. It is an area of family dysfunction.

In the example above, if Saturn is intercepted, your early environment contained no adequate model of responsibility, authority and/or boundaries. It is important to realize that a child cannot learn discipline from undisciplined adults, who often substitute abuse for discipline. Abuse violates boundaries and denies you full authority over your own body/life.

What is interesting in this example is that those with Saturn intercepted often develop a high level of self-discipline, making their own rules and following them. Although they *march to a different drummer*, they always stay true to their own sense of morality.

When planets are intercepted, you must *figure out* what they mean and how you should use them for yourself. Very often that means that the function of intercepted signs and planets must seemingly be *remembered* from a previous incarnation . . . which brings us to another phenomenon of interceptions.

Problems and Solutions

We have long been accustomed to thinking of reincarnation as linear, but interceptions appear to deny that. Positive interceptions seem to indicate one who *comes from the future*—from the next age (currently Aquarius). Natives seem to be *ahead of their times*, especially in the intercepted area. They are more *impersonal*—meaning that their influence is to be *on the world*, more than on any particular individuals. These are the people who will lead humanity into the next age. That leadership is, by nature, a consciousness raising activity.[1]

Correspondingly, negative interceptions seem to come from the last previous age (Aries). They are *behind their times*. They came into a dysfunctional family environment so severe that it held them in a *survival mode*, preventing their spiritual development. Feeling powerless, they become *energy parasites* who live by draining their hosts, through emotional manipulation. The best *host* is one with a positive interception because his or her power level is higher than the norm.[2]

---

[1]This may or may not look as we expect. A prime example for the late 20th century is O.J. Simpson. Whatever one thinks of him, he contributed to the general consciousness in two ways. His trial called major attention to corruption in law enforcement and to issues of spousal abuse. With or without intention, he affected a large segment of world thought.

[2]If you have someone in your life who constantly provokes your emotions—makes you feel anger, grief, even sexually aroused (without following through)—you are dealing with one of these parasites. They must be removed from your life for the sake of your health, your peace of mind, and *your mission in life*.

If you doubt the last statement, consider this: how powerful must a sign or planet be if it is to function unconsciously—which means without attention. Ordinarily it is the attention given us, and our parts-of-being/planets, that *feeds* them, allowing them to live and grow. But intercepted areas are largely ignored, overlooked, even denied. They have to function without attention for many years, as they await their time. They are like valuable assets, put into the back of the closet or the bottom of a drawer and forgotten. They can do little for us until we bring them out of the dark and into the light. Even so, they often act like *emergency reserves.* In crisis, we call on them spontaneously and they answer the call. Consequently, we often seem to be/have *crisis personalities.* Noticing what we can do *when we have no time to think* is the first step in true self-awareness.

Until then we struggle with issues described by the intercepted signs and planets. The struggle will be focused into the house polarity in which the interception resides. The basic issues are:

First-Seventh—Self-image
Second-Eight—Self-worth
Third-Ninth—Belief System
Fourth-Tenth—Need-Response System
Fifth-Tenth—Action-Reaction
Sixth-Twelfth—Cause-Effect

It is common to incur resistance from others, particularly in the affected areas of life. There are several things natives need to know about that resistance:

1. These *attacks* are not personal. They are not attacking *who you are.* Instead they are attacking *what you are.* The resistance is a resistance to change, growth, enlightenment.

2. They are not karmic in nature. You have *graduated* from the karmic wheel. Neither you, nor any action you took, caused this resistance. It is a simple reaction to the *light* which shines through your life, to the gifts of healing and teaching that you offer.

3. While you may learn and/or heal, you are not here to learn anything or to overcome any *malfunction* (physical or otherwise).

4. Neither were you sent to specific individuals. Instead, you are here to teach and to heal *the world.* Your task is not to *save* or *rescue* anyone. It is to be a living illustration of how to live a free and empowered life.

Once you truly understand the source of resistance, it loses its power. The next step is to set boundaries around your life, or to get help from someone who can protect you from attack. Some helpers are incarnate. Some are discarnate. It matters not whether or how your protection comes. It only matters that you realize the need for it and act accordingly.

Until you do, intercepted signs and planets cannot function at optimal levels. Ignored or overlooked, still they rush to your aid when the need is desperate. Given no attention, still, they do not die.

Largely unconscious during our early years, the function of intercepted planets is often erratic, seemingly undependable. Still, upon reflection, we can notice that they do function, and very well, in crises. (Not unlike the way a pounding heart gets your attention.) This can be the basis for recovering them—for making them conscious—for *bringing them out of interception*. *What you can do when there is no time to think*, you can also do when there is time to think. It is merely a matter of retraining.

The Intercepted Life

The great realization to be made is this: born outside the general consciousness, we must learn to live there. We were not meant to *fit in*. Leaders never are. Neither are we meant to finance our lives in the same way, to have traditional careers, to live by the accepted *scientific* or moral standards. We are here to lead the way into the next age. To that end we are *Possibility People* living out previously undiscovered human potential.

The great realizations of our lives must be:

- That we are not here to suffer, but to heal our own suffering, to overcome.
- That we are not here to learn, but to teach, by word or by example. There are many ways to teach.

In the final analysis, our greatest effect is not so much what we do, as how we do it. Our greatest teachings and healings will lie in the way we live our lives. We are the living example of what humanity is meant to become.

Such lives can be lonely. Often few of our relatives or peers understand us. We may encounter resistance in our relationships and careers because others are often fearful or jealous of the power that they sense in us.

However, even as we experience deeper sadness than others, so also are we capable of greater joy. When we learn to live as we were meant to do, without self-judgement or criticism, we find that we are more creative, wiser and/or generally more gifted than those around us. We can have a sense of accomplishment *not of this world*, knowing that we will leave the Earth a better place than we found it.

It is for this that we accept the challenge of living such an extraordinary—or *odd-looking*—life. We did not come to suffer, but knowing we faced hardship, we came anyway. Entering this world, we were *dropped into* a world consciousness significantly lower than our own. At first, we thought that we were *wrong*, that we should change to fit current standards. But the metaphysical message of this book—dedicated to seekers everywhere—is this:

We are not less than those around us.
We are far more.
We are what they will one day become.
But—only if we lead them.
Only if, by our lives, *we show them the path and how to overcome its obstacles.*

The Intercepted Sun

Intercepting the Sun buries Spirit and Identity deep in memory, under layers of conditioning so that it is seldom or never seen. Sometimes mistaken for a lack of self-image[1], it is rather an unidentified Self, an energy-quantum designed for a purpose unknown at the time of birth and/or unacceptable to the adults who surrounded the birth.

The Sun represents our innate sense of spiritual identity and heritage. The energy source for our life, it must remain operable, no matter how secretly, if we are to survive. All else is molded around its core. It is the *impulse to incarnate*, the sperm which quickens the physical seed to create the synthesis of body and spirit that we call human. To function from the depths of an interception, the Sun must be extraordinarily strong willed—not headstrong, but heart-strong.

The difficulty it has is that, going unseen, it cannot be mirrored. Although we know quite well who we are, we cannot know what we *look like* to others. We can never be certain what response or reaction we may get from them. Sometimes they do not see us at all, ignoring us, our feelings, wishes, or needs. At other times they seem to see part of us, perhaps recognizing our existence within the context of our gender, social role, or family, while missing our individuality entirely. Still other times, they seem to see something quite different from our personal reality.

Especially during our early years, other people's reactions to us have little connection with our actions. While most of us learn sufficient social skills to function in society, we

---

[1]Self-image is an environmental construct based on what the adults in our childhood call us, and what they say that we do or should look or be like. It comes from the first house, and its exemptions (what we are taught that we are not, or should not be) in the seventh house.

all get an occasional strong negative response. These come from people who sense our innate (although seldom fully conscious) power. Assuming that we will use it as they would, were it theirs, they become defensive. Some even go on the offensive, making us the target of unprovoked attacks. This leaves us puzzled as to why anyone would fear us. Utterly loving, we are usually the kindest, gentlest, and most patient people around. Our only defenses are our faith and our innocence.

The Dynamics of the Intercepted Sun

The Sun is the most focal part of the chart. It represents the spirit of our life, and by sign, the type of energy we run on. All the personal and social planets[1] depend on its radiation, its sense of identity, and/or personal purpose and intention, for sufficient energy and visibility to function at optimum levels. Because it is the power source of the chart/life, its interception causes the entire chart to be underpowered. With the Sun intercepted, all the planetary functions have limited possibilities for the duration of the environmental effects described by the intercepted signs. Often the planets must *take turns* because the conscious (visible) power supply is insufficient to keep the entire chart functioning simultaneously. It could be said that natives have a different power source from the *norm*. Perhaps some draw static electricity (lightening) from the atmosphere, or run on geothermal energy or. . . . Whatever the source of their power, it is unknown in the time-space continuum into which they are born.

On the mundane level, an intercepted Sun refers to an unknown father[2], an obscured (genetic or legal) heritage[3], or any secret about the native's genetic origins. It is something that you do not know about *who you are* without applying some effort to uncovering the secret.

Intercepting the Sun underpowers consciousness, turning it inward. Mercury's observations and questions are focused on the need for self-discovery. Until the *learner* is discovered, learning is difficult. Jupiter then has inadequate data for its calculations. Therefore, it must infer a great deal from the context of life and/or depend on Neptune's memory. An underpowered Chiron may seem to misfile information in our memory banks, so that it is difficult to retrieve. Until Neptune can image the *person* who needs to remember, and/or the reason for doing so, it cannot access all the available files. It will seem to have lost its *password*.

Intercepting the Sun also weakens the ability to get needs met. Until we know who we are, we cannot discover what we truly need/Moon or want/Mars, nor can we understand what is really of value/Venus to us. With these issues unresolved, Pluto is doubly uncon-

---

[1]Moon, Mercury, Venus, Mars, Jupiter, and Saturn.
[2]Where the legal father is not the biological father.
[3]As when a family migrates to a new country and changes the family name to reflect the new location.

scious and lacks materials for construction. Pluto is then relegated to the role of destroyer of survival threats.

Meanwhile, such energy as gets through the Lunar Channel is directed into Saturn boundaries for protection and/or Uranian crises-type adjustments. Life becomes a process of discovering who we are and what we can do by discovering who we are not and what we cannot do. The more forceful of these two planets (by sign and/or house location) will determine the path of progress. More boundaries will force creative growth. More crises will force expansion of consciousness.

The Sun also deals with heritage and personal roles. Retrieving it requires that we change or adapt our inherited roles before we can retrieve our personal aims from the deeply buried portions of the subconscious. Doing this requires that we change the amount of space in our hereditary relationships. Usually this means a Uranian break with our birth family. Always it means severing the psychological connection created by their influence. Until we do, boundaries remain restrictive and traumatic crises recur.

Understanding Its Effects

With an intercepted Sun, self-realization is a life imperative. While the most obvious effects of intercepting the Sun appear in the fifth house and the house(s) with Leo on the cusp, the entire chart will be under-powered. It may take a long time for natives to discover *what they want to be when they grow up*, simply because an unconscious planet is an unpredictable one. All intercepted planets are largely unconscious, and with the Sun intercepted, much of the chart is semiconscious. It is important to realize, however, that this is a technique designed to support physical survival and that it can only be used by those who are *energetically empowered*. These natives can draw only limited attention from the environment because it is hostile to them.

They must have considerable self-generative power to remain in body.[1]

With the Sun intercepted, most of its available creative energy is required to construct a role that will permit self-discovery. The fifth house will describe that role, but, like the identity, it will frequently be mistaken for something else. Meanwhile, the Leo area of the chart struggles for life. Other planets in the interception, the fifth house, or Leo will also be at struggle. Some will learn to function through their polar opposites as though they were fused.[2] This will speed the process of personal integration, contributing to a rising level of consciousness. This *forced growth* may be one *spiritual intention* involved in choosing the environment that we do.

---

[1]To clarify, see *The Nodes of the Moon*, Rev. Alice Miller.
[2]This will be particularly true of planets in Taurus and Scorpio. See the information on signs in *Principles of Astrology*, Rev. Alice Miller.

However, the underlying truth is that such planets must already be fused, and the integration already in process or even complete. What is really being *forced* is *awareness*. Still, the path to self-realization, to discovering whom and what we are, must take *the long way round*. We begin by recognizing certain parts/planets—meaning that we discover how very well they work. Usually we must intentionally focus on them to do so, because with the intercepted Sun comes the tendency to take the self for granted. At first, we do not notice anything unusual about our spiritual powers and abilities, so they can work only sporadically, when our attention is concentrated on some other part of our life. This will be somewhat true of the entire chart because it is required to run on minimal and usually fluctuating power.

> Metaphor: This is like trying to run a modern home with, perhaps twenty percent of the power that homes normally have access to. You may have any number of appliances and lights, but you can run only one or a few of them at a time. Meanwhile, the power is being secretly drained by some machine that is hidden in the basement.

When the Sun is intercepted, *always* look to the Moon, its ruler, sign, and house to see where the power is going. The only person who can pull this much solar power from us is one who is bonded to us. This is usually our Mother. She took our power for herself or permitted another to do so. This may or may not have been conscious, but it always served her purpose in keeping us contained. On the mundane level, she is the only person who can initiate hiding our identity and/or genetic heritage. Occasionally[1], sexual abuse or other violence perpetrated by someone else may create an artificial bond that will drain us sufficiently to hide our ability to express our real self. It will then force us to live almost exclusively through the Ascendant's programming about who we are or should be.

Whomever the perpetrator, the effect on us is like being starved or otherwise deprived of what we need for survival as what we are. It forces us to live deeper in the body than most of our contemporaries so that physical, financial, and/or social survival are major issues for years. It also forces us to divert part of the available energy/power into physical defenses, because, having learned about *energy parasites* too young, we consider their presence *normal*, and consequently permit them to attach themselves to our lives.

Meanwhile, we intuitively know that there is something specific that we are here to do. But it keeps getting delayed because the necessary time or resources are diverted into other channels. Always we must wait, living on Uranian hope that some day we can express our real self, its role on Earth, and the talents that support it. For many, especially those born before the last quarter of the twentieth century, the real life goal could not ex-

---

[1]This problem is extremely rare and would be signified by a large number of degrees of the cusp sign preceding the interception—definitely more than seven degrees. However, the second problem often hides the first one, requiring a level-by-level process of self-discovery. The best way to hide a secret is with a more obvious one.

press until the eleventh house period. Although often discovered at the Uranus opposition and/or the Chiron Return, it had to remain an avocation until after the second Saturn Return and/or retirement. Younger generations seem to *find themselves* at younger ages.

When the Sun is intercepted, the need for distance from the location and family of origin is most critical. Our sense of self was/is under attack by people expected to validate it. As children, the price of survival, of getting needs met, was our innate sense of self. We had to *be someone else*, forgetting who we were, to get our survival needs met. The role we learned to play was the only form in which we would be tolerated/supported. It is that attachment to survival instincts that makes the role so difficult to escape in later life. Usually it requires a series of crises to dislodge it.

Still, we never entirely forget who we are. An intercepted Sun shows an exceptionally strong spirit, a well-formed sense of identity.[1] We know that we are one of a kind, individuals, different from others. The difficulty we have is that we do not know what that *looks like*, and/or what to *call it*. We may not be altogether certain that we belong to this family, this planet, or even this galaxy. With no other conceptual alternatives available, we can only conclude that we are simply *mutant* or genetically impaired humans. Still, we wonder.

The *absence* of the Sun implies a heavier than usual presence of Uranus, because the intercepted Sun must express through Uranus. Only in periods of crisis, when we must *act without thinking*, can the full range of solar abilities express. Then it is that we do the impossible, proving ourselves the quintessential Possibility People. That which is really invisible about the Sun is that it is significantly more creative than the people in our initial environment thought possible. We have characteristics, talents and/or abilities never before seen in our official genetic line. We are all *changelings* in the family nest. Thus we are identified as the *different*/Uranus one, and/or the one who should be different from what she or he is.

Because we are all highly creative, the very *naming* of ourselves as different, or the belief that we should be different, creates crises. Crises are opportunities *to turn around and go a different way*, even to completely repolarize our lives. Consequently, intercepted Sun natives become highly adaptable and learn to overcome even the most extraordinary surprises and shocks of life. Their greatest genius might be called *the ability to overcome*.

The Effects of an Intercepted Sun on Leo and the Fifth House

Ordinarily, we expect Leo and the fifth house to be places where we can shine. But with the Sun intercepted, their natural brilliance will be hidden behind the need to adapt

---

[1]Assuming that the person survived childhood.

to a wide variety recurring crises. When one continually has to *start over*, forward progress is hindered and delayed.

The metaphysical purpose of crisis is that of calling our attention to our great powers of adaptation and how well we overcome adversity. Once the native really *gets it*, that she or he is clearly much more adept at handling the unforseen, she or he can only conclude that it comes from a state of high evolution and the creativity inherent in that. Then the true genius inherent in the placement can emerge. Reversing the trend toward loss, demanding the return of that which was stolen or appropriated by others, the very direction of flow can be reversed. Outflow/leakage become inflow/fulfillment. Late in life, these natives may become highly applauded, may even acquire fame.

Ultimately, every intercepted Sun native becomes a living example of how much humanity can overcome and create/recreate. Lightbearers of a high order, at the end of their lives, most leave a living legacy for the future that will serve many generations to come.

The Appearance

An intercepted Sun always marks us as one who *looks different* from the family of origin. Sometimes it is a difference of polarity, as when a giver is born into a family of takers. Others function at a different *frequency* than their families. Here we see a sane child, born into an insane family, a *quick* child born into a family of plodders, etc. Commonly, it is a difference of *genetics*, physical, spiritual, or both. The hidden genetic relationship to siblings may be that of a half- or step-sibling, or even an adoptive one.

Psychologically, intercepting the Sun shows an attempt, by those in the early environment, to keep it isolated from Uranus. Doing this keeps us contained withing boundaries set by our family/mother. It separates the personal identity from the impersonal one, forcing denial of any Aquarian pursuits—including astrology. Verbally or subliminally we are given the message that moving our attention/consciousness beyond its inherited/earth boundaries carries a *death penalty*. If we are to stay in *this family*, where we will be loved, protected, provided for, we must cooperate. Overtly or subliminally, we are forbidden to transcend our initial programming, for fear that we will discover who and what we truly are. As a result, our real genius is hidden, and its power drained by the need to use Uranus to adapt to less than optimal circumstances.

Because the threat begins so early in life—sometimes even in the womb, always within the first seven years—it is preverbal and not subject to reason. What has been wounded is our Soul. It is that instinctive, feeling portion of consciousness, where responses are automatic and keyed to subliminal cues. The effects persist well into our adult years, often leaving life-long scars. We must learn to adapt our lives to them.

Many of us learn lifestyles that allow us to meet, or at least seem to meet, the standards set up for us, even while keeping our own intentions alive. Our lives always have an unusually well defined look of *layering*. Never is only one thing going on—whether we notice it or not. Often, only in retrospect does the lifestyle of our early adulthood make any sense, even to us. In time, if we are self-observant, a pattern will emerge that points to the spiritual reality that we have hidden—even from ourselves. Only then can the healing of our lives begin. We learn to consciously use the subconscious[1], instructing our internal creative abilities to exclude those cues which trigger *energy wasting* responses.

Self-realization is a *major* issue when the Sun is intercepted. We must learn to recognize our self from the way that life reacts to us. We must also observe the reactions of others to us, and discover that those reactions are based, not on our actions, but on our beingness and role in life. Others will always love us or hate us, based—not on what we do, but—on what and why we are.

Many natives have a strong *visible*/emotional bond with one parent, and an even stronger *invisible* psychological bond with the other. A natural affinity, a bond of love, with one parent may be resented and resisted by the other. That other will then use *the brainwashing techniques* of abuse to interfere with that bond. Often they justify it on the grounds of some genetically-determined connection which exists between abuser and victim, but not with the other parent.

Sometimes jealousy is rationalized by gender links. Here, girls *too close* to their fathers or boys *too close* to their mothers, sometimes attract jealousy from the same-gender parent. Occasionally the issue is family resemblance. When the child looks like one parent and is more compatible with the other, resentment from the parent whose looks we have inherited, can result.

Often the intercepted Sun literally refers to a division between the biological heritage and the legal heritage. It is relatively common for the native's *genetics* to have been intentionally obscured. Sometimes the mother has concealed the knowledge of the biological father, even from the legal and/or biological father. Because of this, development of the child's talents are inhibited. This can be deliberate and intentional by those who know the secret or simply the result of living in an environment filled with the fear of discovery.

Problems with one parent hinder our relationship with the other and/or with siblings, grandparents, other relatives. Occasionally, they resurface in attacks from our own adult children. Such problems are always rooted in our heritage—or at least in someone's view of it. There is some need to keep our real identity hidden. For some reason Mother[2] and/or the family fear exposure of our true heredity. Because they do, the houses, signs

---

[1]That portion of consciousness that is not normally visible. It is the deep *foundation* that underlies our learning, thinking, and understanding. It contains our creativity ad our memories—especially those established early in this life and prior to it. From it emerge dreams, visions, and other spontaneous imagery.
[2]Literally, the person with whom we initially bond.

and planets surrounding the interception are used to contain this information. In time, the very overemphasis on that portion of the chart, will attract notice and we will begin to question just who we really are. More accurately, the question is what is our real *name*, and/or whom do we *look like*.

Family secrets and obliterated information also hinder our adult relationships. A functional marital commitment must be based on relatively spiritual equality. With the Sun intercepted, inequality in the family is always present. There will usually be a difference in treatment between siblings, and/or a difference in *rights and responsibilities* that depends on gender. Such differences are *always*, by nature, abusive.

This *trains us* to expect and attract inequity in relationship, resulting in marriages between people of different *rank*. Whenever one is the giver, teacher, parent, etc. and the other is the taker, student, child, etc. the relationship is out of balance and cannot produce adequate values or meaning in the lives of the participants. Our mates will not give the *audience response* necessary for us to feel appreciated and/or worthy.

When we cannot define who/what we are, we cannot know whom our equals are, what we do or do not owe others, what our rights, responsibilities or duties are. When we do not know what we *look like*, we cannot know what it is that the other sees and is attracted by. As a result, marital relationships or any other versions of partnership are often doomed to failure until later in life. These *failures* have the appearance of failed expectations by one or both parties. The reality is that one or both have *cast the other in a role* that does not match their native talents.

The Reality

The reality of intercepted planets, and especially the Sun and Moon, is not definable in psychological terms. Only astrology has any real answers. Although intercepting any planet eliminates it from our personal or ego consciousness, what it really does is to separate it from its polar opposite. *We cannot function without all eleven parts of being.* Intercepted planets prove that we can survive and function *without awareness* of some of them.

The *normal* means of awareness for humans is through looking at their reflection. This is shown by planetary polarities.[1] The Sun's polar opposite is Uranus. With either intercepted, the initial command would require us to choose between them. In this chapter, we deal with the Sun, so we are *unidentified*. Being unidentified, we are usually required to use the Uranian *genius energy* to adapt our talent—and especially whatever acting ability is conferred by the Sun—to some role prescribed by the family. We begin life, trying to *fit in* within our own family, because we are not what was wanted, needed, expected,

---

[1]See Appendix I.

etc. On the surface, this may be *explained* in any number of ways, but the reality is that we are not what was *ordered*. We might be considered better, worse, or merely different. Much will depend on the adaptability of the family structure into which we are inserted.

Later in life, we may not be the parent that some of our children wanted, and, consciously or unconsciously, they may punish us for that. On a conscious level, it may be blamed on any number of things, including the fact that we have severed our relationship with our own parents. One of the most painful psychological truths of life is that if we have not healed abuse issues with our parents, they often recur in our relationships with our children. They treat us, not as children normally treat their parents, but as our mates and/or parents treated us. So long as we remain willing to accept abuse, it will continue to pervade our lives. So long as we see ourselves as powerless, we will seem to be so. Only when we reclaim our power, refusing to be treated poorly, will this treatment stop.

At some point every native with an intercepted Sun must realize the Self as a conduit for divine/universal creativity/power. We are the vehicles through which significant changes in the general consciousness are made. Very often, we are also the vehicles through which the Creator of this world, restructures and/or re-creates reality, adding new dimensions, applications, and meaning. We are, and were born to be, co-creators of reality. Being invested with such power implies that we are evolved to a state of love, wisdom, and goodness, in which we are incapable of misusing it. In one way or another, each of us is a high priest/ess, a bridge or conduit between the Earth and the Cosmos.

It is this, which has so long gone unseen, largely because the major world religions make no space for such a possibility. Still, it is time to realize that if we are, indeed, the sons and daughters of our god/dess, then creativity is part of our genetic heritage. All that is required is sufficient maturity to use it wisely and well. To really grasp the full meaning of that, may take much time and thought. It will usually also require some work with affirmations, visualizations, and/or rituals to give it enough substance to be fully grasped by our human minds. It behooves us also to affirm that we cannot and will not misuse that power. One way to understand that is to realize our total incapacity for evil.

For much of our lives we have been confronted from time to time with evil acts by others which completely surprised us. We could not, or did not, see them coming. It is time to know that the reason we cannot see evil in others is because there is none in ourselves. We assume others will be as good-hearted and loving as we are, but few people are. Meanwhile, some of them see our power, assume that we will misuse it as they would, and are impelled to attack first. From this we can begin to learn the true value of being *invisible*. It was our *cloak of invisibility* that protected us, that allowed us to survive in a hostile world. At this point, we can then learn to use it with intent.

Finally, having become accustomed to *hiding* in this way, we must *break the habit of hiding* and reclaim the full extent of our power. When we do, the necessity will no longer exist. If we allow others to see the full extent of our power, it will become a deterrent to our former attackers. Again, practice and some form of prayer are required. In the beginning it was our power that went unseen, a denied possibility. The general belief that power was, by nature, evil, made it necessary to hide it until we achieved enough size and maturity to prevent overt attack. After that, it was necessary to acquire enough trust in our Self and its Source to *name it and claim it*, as our gift, our right, our responsibility.

Because of the need to express through Uranus, all intercepted Suns are Aquarian in some way. Their origin is *Galactic*. They seem to come from some distant time, space, or dimension and they live *between the worlds*, acting as ambassadors or mediators. They are also the *divine magicians*, the alchemists and adepts, existing in a world that has forgotten and/or disowned magic and miracles. We arrived on Earth, at this time, to return these gifts to humanity and its children. They are the gifts that some of our children, most of our grandchildren and all of our great-grandchildren will be born with.

While all interceptions have the *feel* of an origin in some other time, space, or dimension, the interception of planets other than the Sun or Moon may show a *mixed* heritage, as though they were genetically connected to more than one planet or system. These may be more aware of the cosmic connection than most natives without interceptions, but they retain a stronger human connection than intercepted Suns do.

The intercepted Sun is always a Transpersonal Being. This term describes one who has fulfilled all personal and social goals (during earlier incarnations)—by the current definition of human. No personal karma can be attached; *graduation* occurred long ago. If other interceptions equal holding a master's degree in LIFE, these hold a Ph.D. They are the *eldest brothers and sisters* of the Cosmos, the teachers' teachers, the masters' masters, the healer's healers. Being the eldest of the groups who have *stepped back in time, across space or dimension* to help in the transition into the next age, theirs is the task of identifying, empowering, healing and teaching those who actually carry the message.

They represent a somewhat *higher* evolutionary state than the main body of Possibility People. Their purpose is not for the masses. They hold a position in consciousness not unlike that of a Mother Superior in a convent, the Guru of an ashram, the High Lama of a lamasery. To reach full aware-

We may say that the Intercepted Sun is seeded from the *Central Sun*, implying that somewhere there is a galactic system to which our solar system bears a relationship comparable to the relationship between Planet Earth and the *local* Sun. It probably implies twelve of these Suns, relating to the twelve possible intercepted suns. It might be equally correct to say that the origin of the intercepted Sun is in a different age or dimension. Always keep in mind that whatever this *place of origin* looks like, any Uranian context implies an advancement that transcends the *local* reality. The only exceptions would be where the birthplace and environment became so restrictive as to cause a *personality implosion*. That would lead to clinical insanity or coma.

ness, it is probable that the Sun must be at least 181° behind the Moon. Less than that the mission will be the same, but will remain sufficiently unconscious to prevent fully intentional use of its powers. They will then affect reality by their presence, but not through specific, chosen, actions.

Although life can be difficult, it need not be. The suffering incurred is entirely a result of an incomplete self-realization. Full self-knowledge, even in a general way, equals complete freedom of choice, and access to an abundant lifestyle. For these, the mark of progress will forever be the ability to do what they want when, and as often as, they want to, with a companion of choice. In the end, they become examples of LIFE's highest possibilities. That is their mission and its goal is to empower the remaining Possibility People.

Intercepted Uranus

Intercepted Uranus buries hopes and wishes deep in memory under an emotional assessment that we have no power to change anything. We can mistake this for a static ego image and/or a restricted energy flow. We may feel that we are in the wrong place or time, in the wrong body or that we have the wrong name. Nevertheless, since it is *only a feeling,* we have no means of making any real changes.

Literally, intercepted Uranus states that sometime during the bonding period, our *identity* was changed. This usually includes a change of family name—sometimes also a change of given name. The physical image is that of having a new birth chart superimposed over the original one. We were born to a particular set of parents and environmental circumstances, but *the big hand in the sky* stepped in and changed them before we learned to talk or think. The original intent of our lives seems to have been changed, with our energies diverted from their destined path. Part of us continues to hope that we may be allowed to return *home*, wishing that we could begin again. Still, very early in life, we learned to ignore the hope because we have stopped believing that wishes can come true.

The difficulty is that, with Uranus unseen, our personal cosmic connection is broken. We *seem* to know who we are, but our perception of self is limited to the current world view about what is possible to us. We struggle mightily for self expression, but the means to achieve it hides in the interception—literally buried by the changed chart.

The Dynamics of Intercepted Uranus

Psychologically, the real problem of intercepted Uranus is a disruption in bonding. Bonding begins before birth with the biological mother and continues until sometime after birth. During this period, the child learns to recognize and respond to feelings by a process called entraining. The child *rides the emotional waves* of the mother, learning responses by absorbing them from her along with its sustenance. If the person to whom we are bonding is changed during that period, emotional shock results. Certain feeling-responses of the second mother will be different from those of the first one. Sometimes the difference is drastic. The child has no means to contrast or compare the two sets of responses because the mental processes are still unawakened. These changes produce crisis that lodges beneath the level of conscious awareness, producing a *feeling* of something *not right*. It leaves natives uncertain of the validity of their responses to life. Later programming will be sufficient for ordinary affairs, but when it comes to making lifestyle changes, the entanglement in the emotional foundations goes critical. Some natives are *emotionally sluggish,* seemingly unable to decide critical matters. Others are *emotionally impulsive*, changing things in anticipation of events that are mere possibilities. Timing appears to be *off.* No matter how well you perform, it does not *feel* quite right.

When circumstances intervene so that the *mother* who carries the child in her womb is different from the nurturer, intercepted Uranus may picture it. Physically, the most obvious cause of disrupted bonding is the infant adoption. Alternatively, a very sick child, or the child of a sick mother, may have a nurturer different from the in-utero bond. A mother with another child who is ill or severely disabled may give the care of a healthy infant to someone else.

Although one might logically translate this placement as a changed Sun/father/name, and sometimes it does reflect that, neither change means anything to an infant. At that stage, the only significant person is the mother. She is, quite literally, our lifeline. She provided our passageway for entrance into incarnation, and for some time after that she is our source of tangible and intangible nourishment. We have no sense of separation from her; she is our life. If she is changed, during this period, it changes our sense of self, superimposing a second *self* over the original one.

Understanding the Effects

The *picture* presented here is that of disconnecting Uranus from the Sun. In the *normal* course of life, the Sun provides a Solar Identity—meaning that we see ourselves as Earthlings. Uranus provides the possibility of transcending world consciousness to achieve a galactic, and later a cosmic, identity/citizenship.

Each of us incarnates with a personal goal shown by the tenth house and an impersonal goal shown by the eleventh house. *Normally,* we cannot achieve eleventh house goals without fulfilling tenth house goals first. Intercepted Uranus shows that our early environment ignores the possibility of having an impersonal goal. We begin life in an environment with a world view that ends at Saturn, bound by law to Earth.

The adults who comprised our world during the developmental period held a limited vision of human possibilities. They were unusually earthbound and had no interest in, or awareness of, galactic citizenship or eternal life. They were absolute pragmatists who dealt entirely in consensus reality, considering hopes, wishes, and dreams impractical—maybe even immoral. *Color blind*, their world was distinctly black and white.

In mundane terms, the Uranus-ruled eleventh house usually functions as the "if I had a million dollars . . ." placement. Eleventh house factors are usually delayed until after completion of the social goals of career, marriage, and raising a family. Here we store our hopes and wishes, deferring them to *someday*.

Hopes and wishes are *weak energy* ideas that must be compounded by repetition or group focus if they are to accumulate sufficient energy for creation. With Uranus intercepted we learn that these things are *impossible*, or improbable, and that our time and energy are better spent on something practical and achievable.

As with an intercepted Sun, self-realization is a critical issue with this placement. When the Sun is intercepted, we cannot see *who* we are, or what we *look like*. When Uranus is intercepted, we cannot see our *point of origin*, and are uncertain of *what* we are. Often adults who do not realize that infants arrive with a complete personality, obscure it. In others, the change has seemingly been accidental. *Accidents* are probably adjustments made by *cosmic guardians* to compensate for unforseen changes in earth environments.[1]

The Effect on Aquarius and the Eleventh House

Generally, Aquarius is the place in our chart where we are most unique. It is meant to be a place where we can invent or reinvent our selves. In that part of our lives, we are in touch with universal elements, from which inspiration comes. Here we hope to exceed *normal* expectations. However, when Uranus is intercepted, our Aquarius areas are so busy adapting to one crisis after another than there is no time to reach beyond the expectations of the adults in our childhood. Role-playing becomes a survival tool and we are required to play so many roles for so many different people that we sometimes lose sight of whom we really are.

Meanwhile, the usual hopes and wishes of the eleventh house are scattered to the winds. With Uranus intercepted, we have so little hope of changing anything, that we may give up wishing for anything more. Around mid-life a major crisis may intervene, freeing us from the demands of those who ruled our earlier years. After that our impersonal role will emerge, and finally, we will know whom we were born to be, and our intended role in the world.

---

[1]In such cases, it might be said that the *probability line* was diverted in some unpredictable way.

The Appearance

Remember that any person born with an intercepted chart has a *spiritual origin* that is outside the consensus reality. Under normal circumstances, intercepted Uranus natives would be invisible to their parents because we *run on* a different frequency than theirs. We require an *adapter* if we are to live in their world. This is the cosmic reason for the new chart, as symbolized by a new mother. The second bond is the means by which our energy is *stepped down* sufficiently for us to stay visible in the new environment. The effect is like putting blinders on harness horses to keep their attention focused into a narrower than normal range. It cuts out those perceptions that most humans pick up *from the corner of our eyes,* preventing us from being *distracted* by objects existing beyond the prescribed visual range. Occasionally it will take on the physical aspect of tunnel vision.

Still, because of our true evolutionary level, we continue to pick up subliminal clues to the invisible realm. Sensing other possibilities and probabilities without being able to see them, we must choose between the evidence of our eyes and the evidence of other senses. We spend much time trying to analyze life to learn which perceptions are valid and which are *merely imagined.* Only in crisis, can we function *with blinders off* and access to the full range of information available. In situations where we must act *instinctively,* without time to think, we are free to function with full consciousness. Thus, intercepted Uranus usually develops a crisis personality.

From the astrologer's viewpoint, with Uranus unavailable, Neptune and Pluto remain nearly catatonic. Only human evolution can make them personal and accessible to us. Until the interception containing Uranus opens, they sleep and dream behind the facade of your life, sometimes moving restlessly, uneasily, unable to penetrate those solid Saturn walls.

Neptune is both the beginning and the end of human consciousness. Neptune communicates in images. *Neptune* is *our imagination* and it is Neptune, trying to get our attention that keeps distracting us, confusing perceptions. It struggles to extend our imagination to include new possibilities for Uranus to hang its hopes and wishes on. This will allow accumulation of sufficient energy so that we can rebel against rigid Saturn limits.

If Neptune can create enough irritation, the foundations beneath those walls will dissolve. They were, after all, built on sand. Meanwhile, the frustration of intercepted Uranus bruises your head, your hands, or your feet as you *bang your head against, slug or kick* ego beliefs that have solidified into Saturn walls. Bloody and battered, natives often stand waiting for some intervention, some sign, that it is okay to break out of the past and claim their Uranian future. The problem we face is that these are transpersonal boundaries—not personal ones. They are not about what we can be or do, individually. They are about what is possible to any/all people. An obsolete consensus definition of human rights, aptitudes, or values stands between us and self-awareness.

Meanwhile, Pluto stands by, like a faithful servant, awaiting notice. At the mundane level, Uranus represents change through evolution and Neptune through attrition. Pluto's method is different. By using his ability *to split atoms*, he frees energy for new creation. He then *fuses* elements like a cook or alchemist, creating something entirely new from the energy-essence given up by the *old*. He works completely in the world of energy and can bypass the physical world. This means that, with the consciousness of Pluto we can bypass the problem of dysfunctional Uranus and Neptune. If we can retrain ourselves to remove attention from (ignore) the apparent hindrances, they will dissolve. Meanwhile, we can begin *renaming* and/or redefining our lives, doing a general overhaul to the entire ego structure. At some point, the power shifts, from ego structure to identity structure and we call the process a rebirth. Literally the process uses the *power of the word* to transcend Uranian difficulties with change and bypass Neptune's *visual/imaging* problems. We stop trying to change what is, pitch it out, and recreate life. This requires a high degree of intense willfulness, a new kind of blinders and more stubborn insistence than most of us can summon alone. Therefore, it often requires us to ask for assistance from other powerful beings.

Applications

The interception of Uranus is particularly significant because the Uranus principle rules interceptions in general. The planet defines our ability to transcend ordinary Saturn limits. It permits us to *break* certain scientific *laws,* by working in and through the invisible realms outside consensus reality and the general consciousness. Uranus signifies the possibility of magic and miracles working through *everyday* events. Its sign, Aquarius, is the bridge between consciousness and unconsciousness and the point from which the conscious realm can control the unconscious one. Until we recognize this, the unconscious will randomly disrupt our lives.

Historically, Uranus and Aquarius have been relegated to the realm of unreality, assumed to be impossible. More recently, the Uranian functions have begun rising to the surface of human consciousness. They presently reside somewhere between *impossible* and *improbable* in the general consciousness. We, who have the capacity to take an extended view, are aware of a subliminal struggle between two groups of beings, both existing outside the range of the general consciousness. One group is holding firm at the levels prevalent in the late Aries to early Pisces Ages. These are *digging in their heels*, attempting to *guilt* humankind into remaining within certain outdated religious traditions. The other group carries the *Mark of the High Calling* and is on earth at this time to present the possibilities of expanded awareness to the general population. These are the *seeders* and *midwives* of the new Age of Aquarius. Most have had to struggle free of the almost overwhelming effects of birth into an environmental consciousness that did not believe in their existence or their abilities.

Perhaps the most significant role of Intercepted Uranus is that of *Symbolic Possibility Person* They present a clear image of the exact dynamics that all persons with intercepted charts face. They clearly display the struggle to regain our original sense of self, after years of training in the consensus definition of homo sapiens. We are *changelings in the family nest*, and the reality pictured in the fairy tale *The Ugly Duckling*. Taught *duck values*, *duck ideals*, and *duck morality* we cannot begin to understand what is *wrong with us* until, one day, we find the place where swans normally live. Suddenly we discover that we have abilities that far transcend the limits of the *duck world*. We must do a great deal of conscious adjustment before our *duck ego* will let our *swan spirit* live its natural lifestyle without nagging voices in our heads.

Usually, by the time we discover other *swans*, we are married to a duck who complains bitterly every time we *swim away* or *fly too high*. She or he will resent and be jealous of our *swan friends* and try to separate us from them by any means possible. She or he will hate and criticize *swans*, declaring them to be immoral or insane. Mates use any means available to clip their *swan's wings,* even accusations of coldness and lack of love.

The Reality

To continue our analogy, our *ugly duckling* has a unique ability. The truest Aquarian of all, s/he can live between the *duck world* and the *swan world*, and work in them both. She or he can identify with both views and this gives natives an amazing ability as translators and/or transducers. These are the truest alchemists of life, with the ability to change matter to energy or energy to matter at will[1]. More than that, they can adapt situationally by adding or subtracting energy/substance at will.

Natives are living symbols of rising consciousness, imaging the struggle to express new possibilities. Their lives are the prophecies that make the future possible. The most important decision they will ever make is to consciously live in some space that is neither the *duck world* nor the *swan world*, but includes them both. Living outside space and time, they are true galactic beings, and space travelers incarnate. It is their task to link history and future possibilities, taking us from *where we were* to *where we are intended to go*. Required to live in the moment, constantly translating reaction into adaptation, they may look like chameleons. That is a special talent given them for survival in multiple dimensions.

Their lives often show two, or more, entirely different, versions of everything. This can apply to careers, significant relationships, talents, home locations (even dual citizenship is possible)—just about anything and everything. We might call these expressions

---

[1]Uranus in Taurus may be the truest version. They are literal shape changers, capable of presenting themselves as ducks in the duck world, as swans in the swan world. If they begin pushing their boundaries, they may discover a wide variety of shapes and a diversity of worlds.

of different probabilities. Sometimes they are done in parallel, other times in series. It matters not.

Our greatest survival asset is the ability to focus so tightly as to exclude distractions. It is the ability to selectively ignore our environment at will. The most important question we face is what our definition of survival will be. We must consciously choose the quality of our lives, deciding where to permit moral or scientific *law* to limit us, and where to cross into the realm where those laws no longer apply. It is our task to prove the principle of life that allows us to live "in the world, but not of the world."

When we achieve this placement, we live in a place of power that is beyond judgment. Morality, as we have learned it, no longer applies. Neither does practicality, nor even rationality. Our real *home base* is in another dimension where duality does not exist. We are meant to live the principle of Unity, as applied to Multiplicity. This is the very principle of Creation—one energy, one substance, expressed in many forms or many worlds. Identified with that, we are One Spirit, channeled by dual purpose, into multiple realities. Raising our own consciousness, we raise all consciousness. We symbolize the principle of ONE SPIRIT expressed in many versions of individual form. We are the ONE, living as one (a single unit), Divinity as humanity, a bridge or passageway between God and Man. We are the high priest/ess, a visible representation of our invisible Source. Ours is the task of bringing Divine words to Humanity and of lifting the prayers of the people up to their god/dess.

Intercepted Moon

When the Moon is intercepted, the Soul and its directing principle are buried under layers of conditioning. The effects can range from hiding the Moon behind clouds to that of a total lunar eclipse. We can mistake it for a lack of feelings/emotions, and/or a lack of direction. An intercepted Moon gives the appearance of a damaged connection between spirit and body. The Sun may pour too much or too little energy into the body, creating energy imbalances. Deciding what we need for physical maintenance will be nearly impossible. With physical survival continually uncertain, spiritual growth is inhibited.

The Moon represents the *passageway* or *blueprint* for the Solar Energy in/as a body, on earth. It is the place where spirit/energy is converted to visible form/matter. It *looks like* a canal into which energy pours at one end and substance exits at the other. Somewhere in the passage, the invisible is converted to visible form. More literally, the intense Solar Energy is transduced into a form suitable for Earth habitation. When the Moon is intercepted, the conversion is difficult. It is like trying to fill a water glass from a fire hose. A great deal gets spilled, creating free-floating energy which attracts psychic parasites.

With insufficient energy flowing through the channel, physical health may be affected. Poor health or addictions may mask the inability to care deeply. These become the explanation or excuse for our inability to determine what we need or how to get it. More often we lack the necessary energy, focus, concentration or passion to create our lives in a style that supports our spiritual purpose.

Probably the most difficult part of dealing with an intercepted Moon is that there is no overt activity designed to *steal energy* from the natives. The interception marks a *sin of omission*, not something perpetrated against them.

The Dynamics of the Intercepted Moon

Although we call the Sun and Moon planets, they are no more so than the Ascendant, which holds equal standing with them. Symbolically, the Sun is the Divine Source of Life and the Earth/Ascendant is the place where it becomes manifest. The Moon has a completely separate function from the planets, which represent energy *rays* or applications. Her only real task is to convert Spirit to Form. She is the lifeline, the umbilical cord, the silver cord, which keeps us *plugged into* our energy source. When she is hidden, we are not *unplugged*, but we appear to be because the *line* is buried under conditioning so that we may not *see* it. In the process, that line may have become constricted without our conscious awareness.

When this happens, the Saturn boundaries intended to focus and direct energy into our body and lifestyle, become a limiting factor. Consequently, we must learn how to get energy over, under, or through those boundaries before we can experience personal growth. In the most severe cases, even physical growth may be limited.[1] More often it limits *social growth*, keeping us at survival levels of income, in *poor* housing and dysfunctional relationships.

Our means of knowing when and how much solar energy we need for maintenance is our feeling structure. We feel a need and reach for (e-motion) its satisfaction. With the Moon intercepted, the body cannot consciously know what it needs from the Spirit because the emotional structure is untrained. Keep in mind that feelings are pre-verbal. Learning around feelings and emotions must be *absorbed* experientially, largely before the senses are fully developed, and almost entirely before the development of language. We learn to recognize the body's messages by a process of *entraining*. We *ride* our mother's feelings as they emote until we become accustomed to what feeling requires what response. Until we leave the womb, primitive feelings such as hunger, thirst, pleasure, pain, affect both mother and child simultaneously. Normally, for some time after birth she remains connected to us sufficiently to recognize and respond to our needs as easily as her own.

When Mother's feelings have been closed off from us, we cannot entrain them, leaving us unbonded. We do not learn what our feelings mean or how to correctly respond to them. In addition, after we are born, she must respond to us from her *head* and not her *heart*, because she cannot feel our needs. As infants we sometimes experience more hunger or other discomfort than is good for us. At a deep instinctive level we learn that life does not fully respond to us, that what we can get is restricted—sometimes to survival levels. Even in wealthy families where they give natives a great deal, children often go without the things they most want and need in personal terms.

---

[1]Physically this can be imaged as trauma to the spinal column that restricts energy through the nervous system. When it is severe enough, it can even cause paralysis. Astrologically, this resembles negative Saturn-Moon aspects.

Because we have not learned to detect, or to respond to, our own feelings, the emotional *flow* is undirected. Our boundaries do not prevent us from having feelings. Instead they prevent us from *feeling our feelings*, replacing them with trained responses. Natives learn to substitute consciously learned abilities for the *natural instincts* which are inborn. Mercury's perceptive function may then overdevelop its observational skills, producing an exceptional talent for *reading* faces, body language, etc., as a means of knowing how to respond to others.

Jupiter then gets tied up, trying to *figure out* how the native is *supposed to feel* and/or respond to environmental stimuli, leaving little *processing time* available for thinking about abstractions like the meaning of life. Over time, Neptune memory may take over some of this work if natives learn to *tune-in* feeling-response sets from others and their mental stress will decrease. Even then they may seem inconsistent to observers, because they *borrow* from too many people.

Meanwhile, trapped feelings continue to irritate the body. L*earning disabilities* or *behavior problems* often develop as a stress-response to the necessity of using the learning function as a substitute for the *genetic* or *species* information otherwise absorbed from Mother. The effort required to decide this logically (through Mercury) may cause us to lose interest in it and/or it may interfere with other learning processes.

The *absence* of the Moon implies a heavier than usual presence of Saturn. An empty, outlined, space will magnetically draw considerable attention. It cannot go unnoticed, but may take time to understand. When the Moon is less visible, her polar opposite, Saturn, becomes more visible, as the Intercepted Moon tries to express through Saturn. Very often, when we cannot bond to Mother's need-responses system, we bond to her Saturnian limits instead.

Generally, Saturn can be interpreted as the things *we cannot do*. More literally it is a point beyond which we cannot go *without raising our consciousness*. It is a limit only if we believe it is. The frustration of being unable to get certain areas of life *plugged in* properly, forms *boundaries*[1]. When the Moon is intercepted, we may conclude that we are limited, because we cannot concentrate sufficient energy or resources for creativity, especially within the interception. When/as we talk about our *cannots* and our *failures* we reinforce these boundaries so that they hold us in check for a long time. We say that we lack talent, energy, time, means. The real problem is that we lack the capacity to energize our needs and desires into a form that can attract the substance necessary to fulfill them. Sometimes we say that the *price is too high* because we have only enough energy for one creation or activity so we have to choose between them. For example, we may conclude that certain types of relationships, especially sexual ones, and spiritual growth are mutually exclusive.

---

[1]The limits referred to are *personal limits*, not space boundaries.

Because the environment is designed to *overwork* Saturn in certain areas, the Uranian function often becomes quite active. Remember that the interception marks one with an impersonal purpose. This makes help available. It often comes from Uranus, who periodically *breaks* the Saturn boundaries, permitting floods of grief, anger, pain, or other feelings to pour over us, washing away inhibitions and setting us free.

When logic must replace *instinct*, it is natural to assume that the supply of good is limited, and that it will be balanced by the not-good. This keeps natives struggling at survival levels. The effect on Mars, Venus, and Pluto inhibits our ability to know what to keep and what to let go. So much energy is syphoned off into managing relationships with others/society, that little is left for creativity. The best talents in the chart may go undeveloped for years, because insufficient attention is available for the necessary personal assessment required to discover them.

Neptune's task will then be to erode whatever obsolete constructs[1] we possessively hold. This can trigger a surge of feeling that simply overwhelms our Saturn boundaries, dissolving them.

Effects of Intercepting the Moon

An intercepted Moon marks an unbonded child.[2] Without extraordinary intervention from the *invisible realm* or an incredibly strong spirit, such a child could not survive. Still, most do survive, emotionally *crippled* and largely powerless. It is as though there is a huge void where ordinary feelings should be. In reality they do have feelings. They simply have difficulty recognizing and expressing them, so their feeling-responses cannot produce the satisfaction of their needs. Some stop *needing* because there is no way for them to get what they need. For most, the need to overcome the loss of bonding becomes a major life theme. This leaves natives with almost no foundation for their emotional structure. They lack the opportunity to entrain the recognition of and response to feelings from their mothers and are left with the task of trying to learn how to recognize and meet the needs of self and others through the Mercury function by observing how others deal with them. Since feelings are far less visible than actions, this is a difficult and time-consuming task.

A Moon exists in every chart, even when intercepted and thus unconscious. Without it we could not take visible form on earth. Every child emerges from a Mother/Womb, but not every child is properly bonded or gets its (developmental) needs met. The intercepted Moon/Mother is experienced more by touch than by feeling, from before birth to some time after birth. Her psychic presence is clouded or invisible. When the child moves in the womb, she or he encounters the womb only as a boundary on activity. Later, when she

---

[1]Things or ideas.
[2]See *The Soul of Astrology* for a more detailed explanation of the lunar function and the mother-child bond.

or he reaches out, a physical being is there and can be touched, but her emotional touch is limited or withheld. During the critical period,[1] the mother's feelings are focused elsewhere, and she hides them from her child, intentionally or not.

A mother-child bond is designed to allow each to feel the other's feelings. This allows the mother to know what the child needs before she or he learns to communicate those needs. When this ability is damaged or non-existent, the child may have to cry too much and the mother may be driven to distraction by the crying of a child whose needs she cannot recognize or satisfy.

There are various reasons for such events. The mothers of some intercepted natives have used this pregnancy as a distraction to block out feelings. Others have become pregnant at an *inappropriate or inconvenient* time. The developmental problem is that the Mother has succeeded in walling her feelings off from the fetus she carries in her body and/or the child she carries in her arms. Without them the child cannot absorb an adequate feeling-response system with which to face life.

Sometimes bonding was inhibited because the mother's feelings were so strong that they threatened to overwhelm her. As a result she hid them from herself, and consequently from her child. Other times, as when a child is unwanted, the mother intentionally shields her child from her feelings. With intercepted Moons, the quality of care is sometimes excellent, but when the caretaker *goes through the motions* with feelings closed down, the Moon has the appearance of an emotional void in the chart.

Other times, because she is too distracted, she remains detached, even after birth. Consequently, some of these children experience a period when they are left alone—presumably in a crib—for long periods with almost no *psychic contact* with other humans. Occasionally someone changes the child or props a bottle for it, but the least possible physical or psychic touch is involved.[2]

Experience has revealed several underlying reasons. Probably the most common is the death of someone, usually a sibling, within a year or so prior to the native's conception. Hoping to heal their grief, some women get pregnant soon after the death of a child, in utero or later. But, these women often remain focused on their grief, unable to feel joy for the new child, until some time after this child's birth.

Another possibility is that of a child whose conception traumatizes the mother. She may be unmarried or her mate does not want another child, or occasionally she is the victim of rape. After having given birth to two daughters, one mother we knew lived in fear that her unborn child would not be a boy. Her husband was so adamant that she *give him sons* that she thought he might divorce her or make her give the child up for

---

[1]The developmental period from before birth to about age seven, with emphasis on the first two or three years.
[2]This will be shown by additional intercepted factors.

adoption should it be another girl. The son she gave birth to has both Sun and Moon intercepted.

In such situations, some mothers struggle to create the bond at some point after birth. Others experience the frustration of not knowing what their crying child needs. How severe the soul wound is depends largely on how long Mother remains numb, and on whether someone else can provide a degree of bonding experience.[1] Even so, these natives have problems with feelings and/or emotions for years. Because they cannot feel (all of) their own feelings, they may not have much tolerance for other people's feelings, finding them irritating or confusing.

Some natives are attracted by emotional states in others, based on curiosity. Lacking the necessary consciousness of boundary-setting ability, this can lead to unwanted responses. Consequently, they usually distance themselves from others, emotionally and/or physically.

An apparent paradox is connected to intercepted Moons. Many enjoy, feel the need for, or are addicted to, sexual experience. Sexual activity is the only opportunity adults ordinarily get to experience the feelings of another in the same way that infants experience those of their mothers. When we are aroused sexually, our boundaries begin to collapse. If we experience a climax, they drop entirely and the two auras, the two emotional bodies, merge. For a little while we can feel each other's feelings and they are indistinguishable from our own. Their needs and desires become ours. For the intercepted Moon native, this can be amazingly exhilarating, because, during that time they feel whole in a way that they have no other means of experiencing.

The Effect on Cancer and the Fourth House

In any chart the Cancer areas are intended to experience a great deal of growth, but when the Moon is intercepted, growth will be *stunted* and/or delayed until the Moon is freed from the interception. Meanwhile, most of the consciously available energy is poured into the fourth house of family,[2] shelter, and personal safety. Simultaneously, free-floating energy becomes a *feeding source* for others toward whom natives feel a sense of duty or obligation. Remember that intercepted planets must function through/as their polar opposites. With the intercepted Moon, areas meant to be dependant on Source must function independently, and areas which need nurture experience discipline or limits instead. This equals a limited flow of solar/spiritual energy into personal growth.

Having experienced the birth family as an obstacle to progress, these natives may conclude that *families hold you back*. They may avoid creating a family or erect Sat-

---

[1]Intercepted Moons that are close to the end of the interception may be less handicapped.
[2]Originally the birth family. Later the created family.

urn/boundaries to defend themselves against their mates and/or children. This continues to keep them isolated from the loving experience they most need.

The Appearance

When the Moon is intercepted, it must function through Saturn.[1] Thus, when we cannot bond to our Mother's feelings in utero, we bond to her boundaries. Instead of absorbing her feelings, we absorb her limits *from the bonding period* of our lives. From her we learn that feelings are dangerous, that they must be contained and held in check. This can lead to a distrust of the body, because it is the origin of the feelings. Because of it, any type of arousal may trigger the creation of a barrier between ourselves and the apparent *cause* of the feeling. In this society we learn to blame many of our feelings on others. We say that we feel lonely because some other is not with us, that we feel afraid because they threaten us, that we feel angry because they irritate us.

Wherever there are emotions, energy is in motion, trying to go somewhere, trying to create something in response to our feeling of need. When the Moon is intercepted, a large portion of that energy is diverted into protective barriers, designed to keep us from being touched in our deepest, most tender part. That which we put up the barriers to protect is our spirit, our Sun, our heart.

Understanding that our Soul/Moon is always present is important. We cannot remain in body, on earth, without some conversion of energy to form. When the Moon is intercepted, we hide behind our ego boundaries,[2] fearing the touch of another, even as we shared our mother's fear that her feelings would damage us. As the sign polarity opens, we begin to understand that this fear is hers and not our own. When we do, we may intentionally reprogram our feelings and responses, learning to direct the energy they generate into creating the means of satisfying our needs and desires. Then we may discover how well we can parent ourselves.

The Reality

Eventually we come to understand the true evolutionary state of our Soul. When we can survive with a large part of the human survival apparatus closed off, we are amazingly strong. We may then realize that there is nothing in this world or any other that we need fear. Our quality of Spirit is our protection. Here, so much of our *personal* energy emanates to this world, that we have survived on a very small part of it. All we need do is claim a bit more for ourselves, meeting our own needs first. After that the excess *is* for others.

---

[1] If Saturn is also intercepted, see chapter on intercepted polarities
[2] Saturn by house. Third house uses words, fifth might use activity or drama, etc.

Giving may then be done without fear, for we come to the realization that the Moon and Saturn have always been combined. Because of it we have a naturally self-limiting flow. It needs no limits beyond the natural ones, for the needs, the feelings of others can never overwhelm us. If we do not sabotage it with worry and fear, or override it from guilt, an automatic measuring device within us insures that we will never give to others more than we can spare. Then, and only then, can giving become a tool for receiving. Then, and only then, does our giving become an investment in our own good.

As part of the transformative process it will be necessary to face and accept our *negative* feelings, and to verbally deny them power. Whenever, fear, anger, guilt, confusion or any other uncomfortable feelings arise, affirm this:

> I feel (Name the feeling) . It is natural to feel this because I am human, *but* the feeling has no power. (All creative power is in the word/idea which can be expressed verbally, as image, or ritual. Feelings have no more and no less power than we give them by our word/belief.)

Every Moon is a transformer. Most step the Solar Power down to fit a body, a lifestyle. This looks very much like the way that commercial power is stepped down to house current. But with the Moon intercepted, it is as though the connection between the *public power lines* and our personal *wiring* is so poor that much of it is diverted away from our *house*. The small amount that enters must then be *stepped up* sufficiently to run the household *lights and appliances.* The intercepted Moon becomes a step-up transformer, capable of taking a small quantity of energy or substance and making it do work that normally requires a much larger amount.[1] This takes several forms.

The key talent conferred by lunar interception is efficiency. When our energy intake is insufficient for the ordinary way of performing necessary tasks, we develop more energy-efficient methods of living. Many learn to alternate physically and mentally or emotionally taxing activities. By doing so, some can be in a *doing* mode almost continuously. Most have or develop very active minds, capable of designing more efficient tools and methods. At best, they learn to run the visible world from the invisible one, converting weak energy to strong by concentrating thought. An active mind always generates energy and many learn to recognize and use it. Literally they learn to use and manipulate power in terms of physical reality.

One of the more visible aspects of intercepting the Moon confers the ability to *stretch* money and other resources. Natives are unusually good at finding bargains, *coincidentally* finding things on sale just when they need them, and occasionally attracting such things as bank errors in their favor. Very often we give up any recognition of desires, because we are continually at struggle just to meet the needs of self and family. In time we begin to realize that we do not need to recognize needs and desires if we can fulfill them

---

[1]The principle described in the Biblical parable of the loaves and fishes.

spontaneously as they occur. The placement can be beneficial to investments if supported elsewhere in the chart. On the negative side, learning to live on diminishing resources is generally not considered a desirable experience.

Physically, this placement can account for chronic overweight which does not respond to ordinary methods of bulk reduction. In such cases, the early programming of constant neediness creates a physical bias from or like literal lack of food.[1] The being who would, under other circumstances, starve to death, develops a way to get past the lack of necessities. The body learns to survive on less and less, until it can create and store fat from types and quantities of food that *should not* do so, or even directly from the environment. Excessive trauma can aggravate this and deplete the adrenal glands.

In terms of Soul activity, intercepting the Moon pushes us closer to recognition of self as a spiritual being. Our survival instincts (Mars) drive us to seek enlightenment. In the process we discover that there is something more than a merely physical form, consciousness, identity. It is that *something more* that permits us to survive where others would not. When we *lack* (consciousness of) the Moon/Soul, we must shift our perspective. The original way of seeing life is as energy flowing from Spirit, through, Soul, into body. When the connection disappears we are pushed to notice that we are both, and simultaneously, Spirit and Body. Initially we see ourselves as human and created by the Divine. Later we identify as a Spirit expressed through or made into a Body. Finally, we achieve the ability to see that how we identify at any given moment, depends entirely on perspective. When we think we are body, we feel physical needs and must deal with them. When we think that we are both body and spirit, we feel both physical needs and spiritual desires and must deal with both. When we finally discover that the body is only one of two or more available expressions of spirit, we develop the ability to shift focus and live in two or more worlds, almost simultaneously.

Out of that comes the experience of the *Conscious Channel*. When we do not *have* a channel, and are living a planetary existence, it can only be because we *are* a channel. These beings literally experience themselves more as a Soul than as either Spirit or Body. They are the vehicles through which energy, creativity, and/or enlightenment is transmitted from Creator to Creation. They are the keepers of the home for humankind, *Earth Homemakers*, perhaps.

Some chose the lifestyle of High Priest or Priestess of the Goddess, identifying with the Great Mother Image. Some are literal nurturers of children, or the parent of many offspring. These are acting as channels through which spirits may incarnate. Some are feeders of the hungry, and many feed the economy. Most are engaged in the business of birth and/or rebirth.

---

[1] Food is the energy that we believe that our bodies run on. (This talent may have been developed in prior incarnations as Yogi Masters.)

As with any other Moon, the sign placement will describe the form in which energy is transmitted. The difference made by interception is that the focus is moved from our personal life and relationships to the impersonal realm. As with all interceptions, this one marks the impersonal life. Specifically it is the impersonal channel, *feeding* the needs of Earth's children, in form and/or consciousness. This will occur sporadically, even with the intercepted axis closed. It can be a conscious choice, and therefore a much steadier supply for self and others, only after the opening of the intercepted axis.

Intercepted Saturn

Intercepted Saturn buries emotional responses under layers of feelings which sometimes swamp us with *needs* of unknown origin which must be fulfilled before our own. Natives must defer any real goals until they meet the needs of everyone else. Although we sometimes seem irresponsible, our real problem is that we are so responsive to the needs around us that we are overwhelmed with endless conflicting feelings. We believe that our family needs so much from us that we cannot tell where their needs end and our own begin. We can mistake this for poor or nonexistent personal boundaries, because our lives sometimes get *invaded* by psychic energies or constructs which we do not sense until they confront us.

Saturn represents the outer limits, definitions, boundaries or goals of life. These are normally part of the ego and composed of information gleaned from our early environment. Usually we have no sense of boundaries prior to the time when we learn to walk and talk.[1] Planets placed in interception have almost no ego programming. To function from the depths of an interception, they must be *older,* and functioning as a part of the Soul. They are in our spiritual *blueprint* or *schematic*, a part of the directing design for producing our body and lifestyle. With Saturn intercepted, the body/life has been designed for some impersonal purpose. That purpose regulates the flow of energy through life, and sets the goals for it. The affected native seems to have little say in the matter, because his/her goals in life are not his or her own. She or he could be said to have an impersonal ego because his conditioning has more to do with the survival of *generic* life than with personal survival.

---

[1] *Discipline* applied earlier can only be abuse and will be perceived by the child as life threatening.

The Dynamics of Intercepted Saturn

Saturn has long been regarded as a *roadblock* on our life path. Often he has taken the form—or at least the name—of evil forces that tempt us to fail. In reality his function is to set temporary limits which our own growth and development process must push outward. This is graphically shown during physical development. At first our limit is the crib, the playpen, the house. Limits will gradually be extended to the yard, the neighborhood, and finally the horizon. If we look, we will notice their true nature as a moving line which always remains ahead of us, but never actually limits us. It merely shows us the safe outer limits of our current level of consciousness. Always, Saturn boundaries are intended to protect us from being overwhelmed by experience beyond our physical, mental, emotional, or spiritual level of development.

The boundaries represented by intercepted Saturn are unconscious because they are so *far out* as to be more *galactic* than *Earthly* and they blur, even become transparent. We do not learn them from our father, or any other human authority. Instead, we seem to inherit them from our mother in the bonding process. As hers extend beyond the horizon, so do ours. More accurately, the mother-child connection is based on the Venus principle of "like attracts like." In the mean time, the lack of male influence produces over-bonding and your life lesson will be about learning to distinguish your own needs from the needs of others in bonded relationships.[1]

Intercepted Saturn *looks like* a lack of fathering or a lack of discipline. More literally, it refers to a childhood environment in which *limits* were taken for granted to such an extent that no one told this child where they were. We were required to define personal limits through observation of other family members. Without well-defined personal boundaries, we are very aware. We notice that parents have different limits from each other, from their children, from other adults, and/or they may set different limits for different siblings. Observing that siblings have different limits than we have, we do not understand why this is so.

Constructing personal limits from observation is difficult and such boundaries often have conflicts in them that require a step by step realignment before they can be expanded satisfactorily. They function like certain computer problems which state that if conditions X, Y, and Z occur, and neither A nor B are present, then result R can be expected. Depending on the conditions, boundaries may be at a variety of locations. This can look like poor timing, but is the effect of conflict between the *inherited* boundaries and your own impersonal ones. Sometimes your family needs can be synchronized with the evolutionary needs you were born to fulfill. Other times they collide, requiring some intervention from Uranus, Neptune, or Pluto.

The personal function of these three planets is designed for overcoming ego bound-

---

[1] Your mother, your children, and your sexual partners.

aries. Uranus can break connections or relationships that function as boundaries. Neptune simply dissolves hindering circumstances, sometimes quite dramatically by making something disappear from our lives. Pluto *pulls the energy out of* dysfunctional boundaries, confronting their authority with the impersonal power of our pre-incarnational commitment. When Pluto does this, one thing dies and another is born—sometimes simultaneously.

When Saturn is intercepted, the *boundaries* we are confronting are those contained in the current consensus definition of humanity. We are here to be a living demonstration of *inherited*[1] limits—which in terms of current human evolution, are limitless. Here we are offered the opportunity to do the improbable, even the *impossible*.

Understanding the Effects

We need some *stable* boundaries if we are to survive and remain in form. For these natives, the psychological origin of these boundaries is the mother. As always when planets are intercepted, they are actually fused into the polar opposite. Personal boundaries are absorbed from the mother through the mother-child bond. Those boundaries which later *trip us*, or block progress, really belong to her. This may not be apparent because, during the interval between the time we absorbed them and the present, she has moved hers. In the beginning, it was she who felt obligated to meet the needs of everyone else before her own.

Very often this initial program gets woven into, and mirrored by, our adult sexual relationships. Prior to the development of a mature consciousness[2], we will be attracted to others who trigger the memory of our original bond. Thus we state that we *marry our mother.* We literally have a *habit pattern* of bonding with a particular type. In the adult this is usually experienced as sexual attraction because during sexual intercourse we lose our boundaries and are able to merge the two emotional bodies. The better the match between our partner and our inner mother, the more powerful and compelling the experience will be.

When part of our boundaries are derived from Mother, we will be *naturally attracted to* sexual partners that have the kind of limits we absorbed from her. Meanwhile, we have matured and built an entire structure of boundaries, which may have almost no relevance to those original ones. When we are intimate, *we trigger those buried boundaries* and, when they are applicable to our outer lives, they will activate blocks. We are then likely to believe that our mate is hindering our creativity. In reality this other is simply reflecting the limits we inherited during the bonding process. This allows us the opportunity to reprogram that area.

---

[1] We speak of spiritual genetics here.
[2] Generally sometime between the first and second Saturn returns—age 30-60.

It is also important to note that this dynamic attracts intercepted Saturn to partners who have Saturn and/or Capricorn intercepted so that each gives the appearance of limiting progress for the other. The result can be a powerful attraction that has durability far beyond what it seemingly *should have*. The two will usually *hang in there* together until at least one partner's interception opens. After that, this one can help the other, or if rejected, they will usually part company.

The Effect on Capricorn and the Tenth House

In any chart, Capricorn areas are fully matured relative to the general consciousness at the time of birth. Being at the evolutionary state of *elder citizen* from birth, they can feel either *finished* or, more often, as though they have no room in which to grow. With Saturn intercepted, Capricorn can be a place *taken for granted*, ignored, and somewhat stagnant. It does not occur to you that growth is needed. As a result, all attempts to *push your boundaries* are confined to the tenth house.

Remember that intercepted planets must function through their polar opposites, so this Saturn must function through the Moon where we may feel that we *need* boundaries—according to the Moon's sign and house. Until the interception clears, the primary focus of (self) discipline will be at the Moon, limiting the energy output/attention to matters of its sign, particularly in its house.

The Appearance

Intercepted Saturn looks like over-bonding with Mother, ordinarily called *fused boundaries*. While over-bonding is sometimes a mother-problem, this version of it is specifically linked to insufficient attention from the father. In the *normal* developmental process, at some point after birth, the father creates a secondary bond. This is integral to the child's ability to separate from the Mother. With Saturn[1] intercepted, natives have little contact with the father, and/or he does not father. He does not set the boundaries. Mother sets them or we have none in the ego instructions. This has an effect like having them on the wrong side of you. Your ego boundaries are never exactly where you expect them to be. Sometimes women have *male boundaries* or men have *female boundaries*.

With this placement the period of the mother-child bond is extended. During that period, mother was *defended*. Consciously or unconsciously, she was *holding herself together* by force of will because someone/s was draining her energy. Although it may have seemed to be her mate, he merely symbolized the real drain. This points directly to her mother[2], or rarely, to someone who has created a secondary bond through incest.

---

[1]The effect is like a Saturn-Moon conjunction or like a Capricorn Moon.
[2]The native's maternal grandmother. If you are uncertain, ask yourself, "Does Grandmother really like me or my mother?" Intercepted Saturn will surely know the answer.

In worst case scenarios, boundaries never become conscious. This can result in a life-style as a victim or perpetrator of crime because natives have almost no way to gauge the space between me/mine and you/yours. Of these, the daring are lawless and the timid are so law-bound that they fear moving at all.

For most, the lack of limits permits a great deal of progress. We learn how life works and are generally in touch with our personal power. Still, there are recurring experiences of unforseen, unexpected, even unwarranted failures. It is as though we are allowed to progress just so much, or to pursue a particular path just so far, until the *door is slammed shut* and progress is arrested. At such points, natives must *back up and go around* each new obstacle. Progress resumes until the next random obstacle appears. The most important realization we can make is that these *blockages*, these *interruptions to the flow*, are not ours. Because they are not, we can filter them out of our affirmations, visualizations, or rituals by the simple intention to do so. State it, see it, or symbolize it, and the filter can and will work.

The Reality

The reality of intercepted Saturn is that we are truly unlimited. Whatever our solar energy type, whatever our lunar channel, we have a good basic flow of energy. We may claim the rights of the creator-magician as our own, for only a truly powerful one could live in a reasonably successful way, despite the constant threat of interruption in his or her creative work. What is most important is to keep our eyes on our successes. Refuse to claim failure. We cannot fail. The causes of our *failures* are impersonal, even as the causes of our success are impersonal. We can call them symptoms of family dysfunction, impersonal psychic attack, or results of errors in the general consciousness. The best approach is to disown them and not call them at all.

All interceptions mark beings "born outside the general consciousness." Since these *stumbling blocks* are products of the general consciousness, they can be excluded by consciously living outside its parameters. We must accept our role as one *chosen, sent, committed*, and claim the rights of the evolved being that you are. Saturn, in its finest sense, is rights. Our childhood withheld them, but, as an adult, they are ours to claim. This is about choosing to claim our hereditary rights to the *kingdom*. This is about using our authority to exclude unwanted experience.

It is literally about the proper use of denial. Always begin with affirmation. Within each positive statement set a *denial of hindrance*. Put boundaries around your affirmation, visualization, or ritual.[1] This simple technique will clear away all the unnecessary blockages. With it in place, any further limits imposed truly represent direction from our

---

[1]Wicca has something valuable to offer here. Their pathworking begins with the creation of a circle of power/protection.

divine source of power. When that says stop, obey. Understand that our real boundaries are engraved in the soul and can be trusted implicitly. If they forbid us, it is for our protection. They seldom do so—and only when it is truly a matter of survival of body, soul, or spiritual identity.

Saturn intercepted must function through and as part of the Moon. Whatever the sign, the Moon is designed especially for our particular impersonal or transpersonal mission in life. It has a divinely set governor, producing a self-limiting energy channel. The channel/Soul adjusts the energy flow automatically, according to the task set for it, never starving, never flooding, any creative project. All are perfectly attuned to present circumstances, needs, desires.

All interceptions mark *elder brothers and sisters*. Intercepted Saturn may take as his/hers, the title of Elder, for she or he is truly a member of the spiritual hierarchy with a position as *manager* in the *kingdom*. With this position go certain rights and rewards. They are ours to claim and ours to accept. With this placement we are required to be willing to *administer the resources* of a *heavenly estate*, and delegate authority. In some way each intercepted Saturn native is a trustee for the unlimited funds of LIFE. This is the responsibility given to them.

Intercepted Mercury

Intercepted Mercury buries Consciousness deep in memory under layers of conditioning so that only certain portions of it can be seen. The definition of human information processing ability, absorbed during our most intense learning period, ignored much of our capacity for awareness, forcing it *underground.* It required us to sort all incoming information into *files* labeled *acceptable* and *unacceptable* information before we could process it. Certain perceptions, normally handled by the conscious mind, were forced into the subconscious range.

Mercury is the foundation of our capacity to expand awareness. All direct sensory perception, all learning and experience is processed by Mercury. It supervises personal observation and learning transmitted from others, including language and speech. Condensing perceptions and experience into data files as memory, it sets up our internal reference system, like a dictionary and encyclopedia. Intercepted Mercury can take the form of a visual or auditory handicap, severely hindering information processing.

Our entire ability to function in society is based upon Mercury-ruled abilities. It symbolizes the *divine restlessness, the original impulse to reach out*, the energy behind all that we say and think and do. It is the questions we generate and the place where we learn to handle and later to manipulate our reality. To function from the depths of an interception, consciousness must be incredibly powerful because the path of knowledge must go around at least some of our personal, human ability to perceive and learn. In these areas we must depend on memorization/Chiron, computation/Jupiter and imagination/Neptune for social interaction.

Intercepted Mercury refers to some restriction in the learning environment that is similar to, but more obscure than, the problems of retrograde Mercury. Learning capacities go unseen or unrecognized because they fall outside the definition of human consciousness current in the time/place of our birth and early childhood. As a result, a basic portion of our intellect does not get its informational needs met. The *scientific* probability is that Intercepted Mercury runs on a different *frequency* than that of siblings and peers. This forces the child to find other conversational outlets. Depending on the conversational stimuli available, certain portions of consciousness may be overstimulated while other portions will be under-stimulated.

Although natives have high intelligence quotients, there is some frustration that blocks *normal* avenues of learning and/or communication. There are things that we know but cannot express. There are things we need to learn which are not available to us. As a result, energy is *dammed up* in the mind in ways that cause confusion and/or forgetfulness. So much effort is required for everyday function that details may be lost. Alternatively, certain tasks require such a minute portion of our intellect that our mind tends to wander off, leaving our *hands* without supervision. The result looks like poor physical coordination.

Most of us know quite well what we think about everything but cannot express it until later in life for lack of people who will listen or people who can understand us. We can never be certain that we have been *heard*. We may get no answers or the wrong ones for our questions and/or unexpected responses and reactions to our words. We are never certain what to say to whom.

The Dynamics of Intercepted Mercury

When Mercury is intercepted, the thinking process is invisible and thus intuitive, under whatever guise. It is the basic perceptual function that has been inhibited. We have learned *not to see* certain things, or, if we do, not to speak of them. Thus certain areas of consciousness remain wordless without language in which to express.

With Mercury hidden in interception, the creativity of the Sun may go begging, blocked by lack of the words or specific language needed to communicate what we know.[1] When this happens, the entire question of life becomes, "Where is the means to express my self, my life intention? Where can I find someone who can understand what I say, and respond meaningfully?" The intensity of these questions can force the activation of Uranus, bringing sudden and drastic changes needed to shift us into the environment that we seek.

Missing Mercury can hinder Mars' outreach, especially in the social context. We may meet and become involved with people who *need* us but do not want intimacy with us.

---

[1] I remember thinking that there should be some *algebraic equation* that could be applied to all facets of life, years before I *discovered* astrology. Astrology was always present, but was excluded entirely from the conversations of childhood as something not worth serious consideration.

Alternatively we may draw those who want us sexually but have no need, or desire, or room for us in their lives. The inability to express desires can also withhold *substances* needed for spiritual growth, forcing us to choose between social growth and spiritual growth. Most resolve this in linear fashion, finding ways to get some of their desires met socially first, and then, after the social phase comes a time when we can concentrate on our spiritual growth. Eventually this produces an acceptable level of social success.

The usual effect of intercepted Mercury on Jupiter is that of forcing Jupiter to *take over* certain Mercury functions. Under normal circumstances, certain things that we cannot perceive can be inferred from the context of life. When Mercury is intercepted, we must infer an unusually large portion of our information. We learn to *see* what *should be there* as an alternative to seeing what is physically present. We may be so busy *figuring out* some things that we miss the details of our lives.

This can affect our judgment in relationships. We literally see the spirit of people, but miss the ego. Since most people live partly in the ego and many entirely so, we get unexpected results from our attempts to relate to others. We become highly focused on the meaning of relationship, to the exclusion of sharing and value.[1] We will then become involved in partnerships—and sometimes other relationships—whose meaning as a place where consciousness rises (into visibility) partly or completely replaces the opportunity to share space and resources for conservation and production of values. Perhaps intercepted Mercury can always *read people*–but they may overlook whatever qualities are associated with their conditioning *not to see* certain parts of the adults in their childhood.

Intercepting Mercury can also inhibit Mars, because we may be unable to name what we really want. Some have been forbidden even to have desires. Consequently our only means of learning in this area is by inferring what we do want from seeing what we do not want.

Notice that this implies some effect on Pluto and Venus as well. A less common version may affect Saturn, if we do not learn to name our boundaries. Poor boundaries affect the Lunar flow and/or Venusian magnetics. Later in life we may employ a boundary naming technique to prohibit unwanted experience.

The effect of Intercepted Mercury on Neptune is to force us to rely on memory for a great deal. Whatever cannot be learned through the available portions of perception or inferred through Jupiter, must be retrieved from the pre-incarnational memories of Neptune. Over time, most learn to use a large portion of the *awake* Mercury function to *tune in* Neptune's files. This can bridge the gaps in our experience, but sometimes comes up in formats that are out-of-date or out-of-phase with the local culture. The resulting confusion can be quite uncomfortable to live with. Over time, most learn to tolerate high levels

---

[1]Meaning is primarily ninth house, sharing is seventh, value is eighth.

of confusion. *The wisest learn that it is as easy for confusion to work to your advantage as it is to expect it to be counter-productive.*

Finally, intercepted Mercury hinders Pluto's magical powers. Magical word power has long been available, but seldom clearly seen and named. Shamanic magic teaches that the power over a thing lies in knowing its name. Genesis teaches that mankind was given dominion over the earth and later tells how Adam/mankind was instructed to *name* everything. Today we are discovering that those things we name good will be good to us. Equally, those things we name no-good or evil also conform to our naming. A group of *scientific religions* now teach practical applications of this principle. What they do not always include is the fact that Jupiter/belief must align with Mercury/words if they are to achieve the full power of their fusion through Pluto.

When Mercury is intercepted, the most common difficulty is that the way we learn to name life is disconnected from the belief system which surrounds us during the language-learning period. Therefore, we may logically know that we can create *a million dollars* by naming that reality, but our belief that we cannot or should not have such a sum, drains the power from the words. For most it is better to begin at a much smaller level, gradually rebuilding our beliefs on the foundation of multiple and growing successes.

This disconnect also has a chain reaction that permits us to have who/what we think that we need in our lives, but not who/what we truly want. Again, Pluto must fuse need and want, but to do it requires a clear and accurate definition/naming of need and desire.

Understanding Its Effects

With an intercepted Mercury, some understanding of the dynamics of consciousness is a life imperative. In recent years many intercepted Mercury natives have gravitated to the personal computer industry because it presents a graphic picture of the *mechanics* of the mental processes. Older natives studied some version of metaphysics and combined it with a divinatory technique which would help them to tap into their own subconscious.

Intercepting Mercury breaks its connection with Jupiter or Neptune or both. When the Jupiter connection is broken, we cannot depend on sensory information because we have learned to disbelieve our senses. This may affect only the intercepted houses, or it may extend to other houses through secondary interceptions caused by having other planets intercepted. This means that some portion of our knowledge must be inferred or gleaned from the context of life. It is something like trying to read a book with unfamiliar words, without a dictionary in which to look them up. Over time we will become exceptionally adept in making *educated guesses* about life, but, until we understand the nature of our consciousness, we continue to make occasional mistakes in interpreting reality.

Living by this method, we are required to depend heavily on a belief system. When the interception is Gemini-Sagittarius, or when it is in the third-ninth house axis, this can be problematical. It definitely points to an exceptionally powerful consciousness, capable of over-riding much of the need for environmental/perceptual information. The difficulty is that these natives creatively produce any reality they believe in so efficiently that it becomes nearly impossible to make large or permanent changes in their lives.

Intercepted Mercury must of necessity be unusually intelligent. Because of this, hiding or limiting the opportunities or equipment for learning, for expanding awareness, can be incredibly frustrating. A few give up and *run away from life*, into a monastic life, or into insanity. Most simply learn to depend on feelings, emotions, and the Lunar Channel for supporting information, from which they calculate the information or answers they need. This forces development of empathic and/or telepathic skills.

When intercepted Mercury refers to a broken connection with Neptune, we have learned that peripheral or subliminal information is flawed and unusable, that dreams and imagination have no substance, meaning or value. Additionally or alternatively some have experienced real events that parents or adults denied by ascribing them to imagination or dreams. In such cases the very definition of dreams may become that normally associated with nightmares, and the child will stop dreaming. Imagination and/or the ability to image will be projected onto others.

This carried exceptional weight because in that environment *everyone knew* that dreams and imagination were useless, worthless, or destructive. Sometimes they were explained as *coming from the devil*. Other times they were ascribed to a *lethal, animalistic subconscious*. The child concluded that having too many dreams, or too much imagination became a mark of evil or insanity.

Some natives simply had a wider perceptual range than the adults around them. As a result they saw the figures or heard the voices of discarnate friends or relatives, of angels, fairies, or other beings which function at a vibratory level different from consensus reality. When adults became aware of this, they denied the reality of what the child saw or heard, forcing the child to replace sensory information with unquestioned or unreasonable beliefs taken entirely on *faith*. In the latter case, very often the experiences were declared evil and demonic and children were forbidden, on pain of hellfire, to see/hear such things again.

Depending on the level of physical abuse or emotional swamping that accompanies it, the child may lose touch with all dreams and/or imaginative experience, or some significant portion of them. It will then be necessary to create other means of getting information that would otherwise arrive as direct intuition. Those whose experiences are similar, but have less impact, may be able to channel this energy into artistic development. This permits the images to become paintings, poetry, or other socially acceptable expressions of imagination. Suppressed dreams may come out as science fiction or other imaginative novels. When the interceptions begin to open, some natives notice that they have been experiencing their imagination by projecting it into novels. A heavy reading habit can keep imagination alive for later use.

Astrology has always been an exceptionally efficient tool for pulling ideas from the subconscious realm into the conscious one because it provides a means of calculating ideological probabilities. With practice, we discover that whenever we can *get hold of* one end of an information quantum, we can assume that the other end is present, even when it is invisible. Any background belief system that gives us permission to delve into the mysteries of life can be combined with astrology's method of calculating information, to direct our questions. Those questions must produce answers—by the natural laws of consciousness.

In today's world, astrology, I Ching, tarot, numerology, etc. might all be compared to computer programs. Each provides a means of getting into and/or working with files of information that are not currently in our personal (the upper levels of awareness) consciousness. Some of what can be reached in this fashion is personal memory. Other possibilities are racial, world, galactic, or universal memory. Any divinatory tool will tap certain portions of the available network of memories. It is our belief that astrology provides the most accurate tool for precision referencing of information from these areas. There is no *good or bad* tool, just a question of which tool works best for reaching the specific information that we seek.

The Effects on Gemini and the Third House

In any chart, Gemini areas represent nearby relationship—those things and persons that are parallel to us. This includes *like-minded* people which are ordinarily thought to include siblings and peers. However, with Mercury intercepted, our perceptual functions *run on a different frequency* than those of siblings and peers. This means that we have a different perspective on life, different interests and different thinking and/or communication styles. If we have intellectual peers at all, they will be found outside our families and peer groups, and outside the third house.

Very often the contents of the third house describes the people to whom we relate as peers during childhood—as Saturn or Capricorn/older people, Jupiter or Sagittarius/teachers or foreigners, even Sun or Leo/highly creative people. The latter may refer to *pretending to think*, rather than revealing what we already know. But when your relate to adults while a child, whom do you relate to when you reach adulthood? Peers-in-consciousness are quite rare until after you discover the correct *language* in which to communicate the wisdom that you have to share.

Gemini also represents questions, and when Mercury is intercepted, we have difficulty finding anyone who can answer—or sometimes even listen to—our questions. This is the effect of its initial *split* from Jupiter. The third house describes whom we initially ask or talk to. However we will soon discover that it has little to teach us. Because Mercury must function through Jupiter, we must teach ourselves, learn from ourselves, and find our own answers. Although we may seem to *figure out what should be in the places we cannot see*, very often answers come intuitively, from Neptune. At its best, this construct will allow us to *figure out* a great deal by tapping into our *internal Internet* for data.

The Appearance of Intercepted Mercury

Intercepted Mercury refers to a child whose sensory abilities are taken for granted. It never occurs to the adults in the early environment that s/he may not see, hear, or otherwise perceive the same things, in the same way, that they do. When they are confronted with contrary evidence, they over react[1] or under react[2]. This is often designed to stop the child from perceiving what the adults cannot, or do not wish to, see. The intention may also be to keep the child from talking about what she or he perceives.

As children, natives discover that they are more[3] intelligent or perceptive than their siblings and/or parents appear to be. The reality is that they can see, hear, or otherwise sense things in a way not currently available to others around them. Sometimes the child inherits his/her perceptual range from one or both parents and discovers it during the period when it is unconscious in the parents. Other times it is drastically different from the family level of awareness. This can produce a variety of effects, depending on the *ages* of the people involved[4], and the surrounding belief systems[5]. The child may learn that this expanded knowledge is useless, evil, a responsibility. It can make him/her unequal, give him/her control, and/or *cause* emotional or physical abandonment. As a result, s/he will feel incompetent, believe that she or he is demon-possessed and/or to blame for family crises, and/or that s/he must always justify and/or forgive others who abuse him/her because they *do not know better or cannot help it.* Intercepted Mercury makes the expanded perceptual function a heavy burden that trains us to focus a disproportionate amount of energy into one of its polar opposites. It forces us to use Jupiter or Neptune to replace blocked Mercury functions.

We are usually expected to *understand* a great deal of irrational adult behavior. Often much of our teaching is focused on statements like, "Do as I say, not as I do." We conclude that because we can see the irrationality and they cannot, we are smarter, stronger, etc. and that this additional gift requires us to forgive them on the grounds that, "They

---

[1]By shouting, with physical violence or threats calculated to stop the behavior, on the grounds that it represents character flaws or internalized evil.

[2]By taking the child's statements as a joke, an attention getting device, an over-active imagination, or in some other way denying that what the child says is connected to an actual perception.

[3]Or, rarely, less.

[4]Specifically on Neptune's sign.

[5]Third-Ninth axis.

know not what they do." We assume that when others attack us, or hurt us, they do not mean to do it. This can severely handicap our survival instincts, retarding their natural protective functions.

Example Blockages by House

1. People don't see me, hear my name.
2. They don't recognize my value.
3. They don't recognize my intelligence.
4. They can't see my needs.
5. They don't see my role in their life.
6. They don't see my function clearly.
7. I have space issues in relationships
8. I have amount issues in my relationships.
9. I have growth issues in my relationships.
10. I am not given the right/ authority to speak.
11. My hopes and wishes are unconscious..
12. My dreams and/or the causes of my life crises are blurred or invisible.

The basis of this is that infants and small children must believe that their parents are benevolent and sane. For the small child, parents are gods. If their gods hate them or hate life (the basic insanity), they can have no expectation of survival and will give up the effort to live. When a child has one or more adults in their immediate environment that are insane, or that are struggling against insanity, some version of blindness, deafness, or forgetfulness becomes a survival imperative. Some will blind themselves to the meaning—Jupiter, and others to the reality—Neptune.

Intercepted Mercury always suggests some version of dysfunctional information processing designed to hide awareness of evil in the original environment of the native. Astrologers may look for one or more parents or grandparents with portions of the consciousness structure intercepted.[1] In some cases, both parent and child are struggling with the effects of evil or insanity in a grandparent. Usually this will follow a matrilineal line. It may have additions from patrilineal lines caused by the principle of magnetic attraction.

The Reality

The human aptitude for learning is the quality that most clearly separates us from the remainder of the animal kingdom. Those familiar with Genesis, may remember that on the *eighth day*, the Creator made a man of *earth elements*, then *breathed into him* the

---

[1] Mercury, Jupiter, Neptune, and/or the signs they rule would be intercepted.

breath of life. Astrology teaches *breath* as a symbol for consciousness. It means you are alive and conscious. It means you are capable of receiving and of giving information.

Breath is most obvious in the Gemini-Sagittarius polarity. It refers to one who learns to teach to learn to teach . . . and the cycle goes on. When Mercury is intercepted, the cycle is broken, because the early environment lacks teachers, lacks anything we can learn. Natives are born into a time-space in which there is no one who can or will teach us the things we need or want to learn. There is no outer stimulus for growth in consciousness. At its simplest, this might refer to a hearing child born into a deaf family. Who would teach the child to talk?

The more common experience is that of a gifted child, a genius or a prodigy, into an *ordinary* family. Sometimes parents and/or siblings resent that child. Other times these gifts go unrecognized or they are ignored by adults who hope they will go away. Occasionally their gifts are perceived and judged worthless, and/or symptoms of insanity or evil. One way or another, the mind *starves* for lack of stimulation. These children can sometimes be a real challenge to parents who must keep their interest or take the consequences.

If natives are to educate their gifts, they must design and follow an original educational plan. Usually the real *career goal* is one that has not been invented, or something not considered a valid career, during the early years of life. Most eventually take up a profession outside the comprehension of those who asked, "What do you want to be when you grow up?" For this reason, it can take many years to answer that question and sometimes the most significant part of life comes after their official retirement from the general labor force.

Most intercepted Mercury natives are born with clairvoyant, clairaudient and/or telepathic abilities. We do not at first realize that other people do not have these abilities. If that discovery has sufficient trauma attached to it, we may *forget* our most significant talents. These abilities then go *into a coma* until some crisis awakens them.[1]

Mercury's interception forces us to use Jupiter or Neptune as perceptive tools. Literally, this means that Mercury must be fused with at least one of these planets. Jupiter fusion produces one who thinks in concepts, rather than in words. It *looks like* a very fast computer because it appears to bypass the process of information gathering required to formulate concepts or define principles from sensory data. In fact, it refers to the fact that the base of sensory data is unusually large and that this information can be abstracted from memory instead of calculating it. When it is fused with Neptune, it is like a computer linked by network to many databases, so that it gives access to larger memory banks that include files originating with other minds in other times, spaces, dimensions.

---

[1] One of the most significant marks of a high evolutionary state is the ability to deal with crisis, and many of us create our lives in ways that demonstrate this.

The Jupiter-Mercury fusion produces an excellent teacher capable of breaking down principles into applications and of synthesizing *new* principles. This type is clairaudient. The Neptune-Mercury fusion produces information from mysterious and usually untraceable sources. It gives you information that you may not understand how to use or for reasons that you cannot fathom. More than that it often produces information from such remote sources that symbols/visions must replace language. It is the clairvoyant or clairsentient.

Most natives are somewhat telepathic. Telepathy is probably an adaptation of clairaudience designed to bridge communication gaps, so it is most obviously Jupiterian. However, it uses Neptune's ability to see, hear, or walk through consensual boundaries to cross the *boundary* created by using physical hearing to limit communication. There are many versions of this, including that of using astrology or numerology[1] to reveal a pathway into the subconscious areas of another's mind.[2] Other versions are described as the ability to read auras, emotions, facial or body language, graphology, even *reading between the lines* of communication.

Intercepted Mercury can only signify one who has learned to be a Teacher and/or a Master. Both are, above all else, communicators with the goal of expanding the consciousness of others. Probably the only difference is in the quality of information or the number of persons reached. These are *students of reality*, relearning the principles of consciousness that make it possible to travel to other realities and to transcend each ending by choosing a new course of study. They teach their *younger* siblings how to transcend the senses. They teach themselves how to transcend time and space. In one sense or another, these beings are all Seers. Most learn to *fly*.

---

[1] Other divinatory techniques would also work, but these are the most obviously telepathic. Other methods or additional skills might pick up information from the Akashic record, etc.

[2] An intercepted Mercury is not required for this, but all intercepted Mercuries have some of this ability.

Intercepted Jupiter

Intercepted Jupiter buries our self-concept under layers of beliefs so that we cannot figure out what we can do or be, where we need to go, why we are here. Clearly we have certain abilities, but they seem irrelevant to the birth environment. In it we have no place to exercise, educate, or use them.

This placement is sometimes mistaken for a lack of intelligence or a lack of mathematical skills. It is not a lack, but a simple mismatch of abilities and circumstances that can make us look incompetent or unskilled. It compares to having a musical prodigy born into a deaf family or one so poor that the struggle for survival precluded such *luxuries* as music. Our greatest talents are frustrated. Until they can be freed, life will be less than it was intended or designed to be.

Jupiter represents our ability to exponentially extend our initial ideas, learning, and experience. He gives us the ability to calculate, compute, or infer information from what is at hand. On the physical plane, he compounds short journeys into long ones. His principle also functions in relationship, expanding the horizons of both as each becomes acquainted with or connected to the other's circle of friends and relatives. Intercepted, that ability becomes an unknown quantity because the family belief system inhibits certain Jupiter functions. It is *understood* that these are impossible or inappropriate to us, by heritage, by gender, by circumstances, etc. Alternatively, they may be forbidden so that we are required by the religions of our childhood to *stay within our limits.* Intercepted Jupiter points to some learned beliefs about things you cannot do, places you cannot go, things you cannot become, because of your birth time or place. It literally says, "You cannot get there from here."

The Dynamics of Intercepted Jupiter

If the Jupiter function were truly withheld, few would live much past adolescence, and no one would get far from home. Education would be limited to very basic levels and life would begin to seep away. It is Jupiter's ability to expand or extend—anything and everything—that gives humanity the capacity to be more than the mammal biology makes us. It is at this level that biology expands into psychology and philosophy, and from there to metaphysics.

Mercury, Chiron, Jupiter, and Neptune symbolize the components of our consciousness structure. Mercury gathers and processes data. The real *computer* is Jupiter. He contains all the *mathematical skills,*[1] while Chiron organizes files and Neptune offers *extended memory* through a network interface. Intercepted Jupiter literally points to a childhood that hid your intelligence, by making you believe that certain things were outside your parameters of being or experience. You may have all the information and intelligence in the world, but with Jupiter intercepted, you initially believe that it is meaningless or useless. This is the effect of breaking the connection with Mercury.

Understanding its Effects

As always, the origin of this is in the early environment. From birth you can see, hear, perceive a great deal, but much of it is meaningless. It *will not compute*. The behavior of at least one parent is completely irrational. What you do not know, because you lack examples to compare with, is that what is going on really does not make sense. The other parent and any other adults around cannot or will not see or acknowledge this. Often the family is so insular that you see few people outside it before you reach school age. Literally you learn that life does not make sense. More importantly, you think that the problem is in you, because you cannot understand the logic of such behavior. It may be years before it occurs to you that there was none. The lesson of this placement is simple: logic does not work on the insane.

Effectively, intercepted Jupiter forces us to use Mercury to handle most information processing. Usually it emphasizes the Virgo side, forcing us to learn from experience what we have *lost* the ability to calculate from known observation. Because we are denied Jupiter, we work far too hard at learning life's lessons and we have great difficulty *traveling very far*. Life has taught us to avoid *jumping to conclusions*, or *skipping over* certain areas. We learned to keep our *feet on the ground* and our *eyes off the stars*.

One of the interesting side effects of this placement is that natives sometimes learn to survive all the stress by cultivating their Neptunian abilities. Because dreams and psy-

---

[1] We use this in the broadest sense. We compute far more conclusions from perceptions and ideas than from numerical data.

chic abilities have not, historically, been considered mental processes, or relevant to daily life, they can sometimes be practiced as a *hobby*.

We can also exercise them under the guise of sleep. Meditating without those around you realizing it is possible; people will think you are asleep. Many intercepted Jupiters spontaneously resurrect artistic or psychic abilities from *memory*.[1] Those things which cannot be seen or inferred can sometimes be *imagined*. Doing so exercises the Neptune function and allows it to help Mercury's overworked perceptions.

Without this adaptation, the Saturn function usually gets overemphasized. We perceive those beliefs that have forbidden expansion as *roadblocks* on our path. These act as artificial boundaries and limits and are convenient *explanations* of why we cannot travel far in certain directions.

For most, the blockages described are not absolute. Very often, intercepting the Jupiter function limits only physical expansion and/or travel so that we cannot accumulate wealth or move far from our place of origin. It is this lack of money, travel, or educational opportunities that seem to withhold opportunities for self-realization and spiritual growth. Some interpret this as *bad karma*, as punishment for some unknown sin or inadequacy, or simply a kind of *physical disability*. What is interesting about this is that most find some means of bypassing these circumstances.

Coincidentally, we meet people who present new ideas to us or we manage to glean awareness from mundane reality. While it does not get us very far down our *spiritual path*, it does keep our desires alive. Over time, hopes and wishes accumulate energy or the fusion described by using physical reality as a symbol for nonphysical reality can uproot the old beliefs. This will *look like* a transit of Uranus or Pluto to the intercepted axis and Jupiter.

Intercepted Jupiter withholds our future, hiding tomorrow from view. We have no way to infer a goal from the present reality, so the future is unknown. Meanwhile, our personal expansion often continues behind the screening interception. Jupiter is the principle of expansion and it will expand even while we are not looking. Unable to affect our external horizons, it must expand the internal ones. Although a transit may appear to activate the interception, in some way Jupiter simply gets too big to be contained within it. It will *break out* of the interception and begin moving outward in a rather Uranian fashion. Alternatively, it may seem to *explode* with Plutonian force, suddenly freeing us from the past.

This can look like a religious conversion. More often, Jupiter is catapulted out of interception by some life and death confrontation, even a literal restoration from death or NDE.[2] The *divine survival instinct* erupts past the ego blockages created by childhood

---

[1]Memories of other lives, the Akashic record, etc.
[2]Near Death Experience

programming or later brainwashing. For a moment, life is *shorted out* completely, allowing us to be reborn *on the other side of* the old limiting beliefs.[1]

With Jupiter intercepted, the need for personal growth and/or enlightenment goes critical, becoming a literal life and death matter. Like all interceptions, this one has a specific, impersonal, commitment. Each native represents, within him or herself the critical need for enlightenment within the human species. Each is a living symbol of life's struggle with static beliefs.

The Effects on Sagittarius and the Ninth House

Ordinarily the Sagittarius areas of the chart are light-hearted, expansive, and thoroughly understood. Here we are becoming more from birth as we continually expand our horizons. However, when Jupiter is intercepted, we may instead feel abandoned and alienated. Here we have difficulty *gaining ground* and while we often have *enough* we cannot exceed subsistence levels without expanding our definition of *enough*. The interception of Jupiter confines him to "last minute" benefits, which may protect us from absolute disaster but give us little more until after the interception opens.

Meanwhile, educational levels and travel are restricted in the ninth house. Always we have accepted some hindering belief as fact. It will only be as we form our own, quite individual, belief system that we can begin to reap Jupiter's true benefits. This placement encourages the study of philosophy, psychology, and/or metaphysics because they are the tools that help us to understand what blocks Jupiter's bounty from our life. But since higher education is usually not available, the native must pursue these studies on his or her own. Each native first teaches himself or herself before becoming a teacher of others.

The Appearance

The adaptations people make to live with *given* beliefs can be quite interesting. Although usually regarded as a social planet, one facet of Jupiter is optimism; denying Jupiter energy entirely is thus impossible. It will always *slip its bonds* in some fashion.

Example: One case that we are familiar with sublimated what he perceived as a *need* for higher education by reading, almost compulsively. Like most people with an overemphasized Mercury, he compiled huge files of information and could discuss almost anything. Still, there were *places* that intercepted Jupiter *forbade* him to go. He held, and attempted to live by, certain memorized bits of dogma, specifically a personal demon. He once told this writer that "astrology is of the devil." When we pointed out to him that the magi who followed the star to Bethlehem were astrologers, he dropped the subject imme-

---

[1] With the current Pluto transit of Sagittarius, the entire world will be confronted with issues of belief vs survival.

diately. Since he was one who enjoyed a good argument, clearly, he knew that his *belief* was indefensible.

Example: His son *inherited* the intercepted Jupiter, along with his father's first name, but with fewer complications. He has spent his life challenging his own boundaries, expressing his real beliefs outside the context of religion. Relatively successful in his career, he fathered three sons, and spent some years as an active boy scout leader. In this fashion he fulfilled the family beliefs without triggering debilitating guilt. Part of his personal crusade involved consciously forcing his parents to face the beliefs they taught him. Both men are dyslexic due to having their natural left dominance forced to the right.

Intercepted Jupiter produces some sense of inferiority. We can avoid this in various ways as in the first example. It can also become a challenge that drives natives to *prove something* to the world. It sometimes causes such a severe arrest in the self-concept as to produce agnostics and atheists. Other times it creates an *anti-belief* reaction, so that natives choose to follow a belief they consider diametrically opposed to the learned one. In an officially *Christian* country, these may choose an eastern religion, a pagan one, or in worst case scenarios become neo-Nazis, Satanists, etc.

Far more commonly they simply ignore the subjects of religion or philosophy, professing an inability to understand them. Still, most lead a highly moral life, run from their instinctive sense of truth. More than most, these live from the basic belief that LIFE is the highest, and the only *absolute* morality. Most understand the value of joy in producing the "life and greater life" mentioned by the Master Jesus. In them, life wells up, causing growth to sprout outside the beliefs of childhood. In time it can reach awareness. If delayed too long, it can produce the confrontations with death described earlier. With the interception open, the expansive concept can function in dramatic ways, producing wealth, fame, or other types of personal expansion.

The Reality

These are the Living Messengers of life and the *unseen angels* in the lives of others. Often found in humble circumstances and rarely aware of their role in the lives of others, still their mark is left on this world. These are the preservers, the protectors, even sometimes the teachers, of other, more visible, *Possibility People*.

Only in the rarest of cases do they become *fallen angels*. When they do, they give that confrontation with evil that some find needful in their spiritual evolution. Always, good finally overcomes evil, wisdom overcomes ignorance, and life eternally expands to greater dimensions. It will do so, even behind the ego belief that faith is irrational and cannot be understood. Students may remember that the original ruler of Pisces/faith was Jupiter and for many, faith is still a matter of unquestioned beliefs, not subject to analysis. For the few, this has forced a choice between reason and faith. For the remainder it manifests as the simple inability to *understand* the beliefs of their childhood *because* those beliefs which they were expected to *take on faith* were irrational and destructive to life. Only when the interception opens, revealing the remembered truths from other incarnations, will they come to understand the nature of that which they have been expected to believe.

Remember that the essence of intercepted Jupiter is that it is split from Mercury. It actually refers to beliefs whose rationale is invisible. In practice it usually points to learned beliefs that are not rational. Because of this, natives sometimes struggle for half a lifetime or more, trying to make sense of their native belief systems. Only when they *travel* to other places or cultures, whether overland or intellectually, can they find a validating reflection for their own internal belief system. In the end, for full, efficient, activation of those beliefs, they must name and declare what it is that they believe in. When they do, they may reach the stars that have always been their goal. Meanwhile, they activate that *search for truth* in others.

Ultimately Jupiter is a preparatory stage, a foundation of understanding, from which enlightenment springs. When Jupiter's understanding of the underlying principles of life emerges into consciousness, it becomes the wings on which we travel to transcend time and space. Underneath all the conditioned beliefs, intercepted Jupiter knows that *space travel* and *time travel* are possible, because that is how she or he got here. The gift, buried under his/her childhood conditioning is that of flight[1].

---

[1] Astral travel.

Intercepted Mars

When Mars is Intercepted, desire is buried under layers of ego judgment and/or conditioning. Most humans in the current time-space, have learned some condemnation of desire. We have lost its original meaning as the energy directive *of the Father*. It is desire, the desire to be, to have a body, to become more than that body, which powers the entire human experience. With Mars intercepted, we have difficulty knowing why we are here. Consequently, we do not know what we want. If we are trained to believe that we want or should want certain things, we may pursue them, but getting them does not satisfy. We are left wanting . . . something, we know not what.

When Spirit incarnates, it does so from desire. Its naturally radiant energy is projected into a human form designed to mirror its Creator. Humanity is seeded from Spirit's desire to become visible, tangible, and real. A *seed* is generated, placed in the *womb* of earth, and nurtured into a form. Inherent in it is the ability to *cause* or *tune in* a visible structure of experience that can be integrated into the personal being, and by extension, into the Divine Being. As physical entities, our point of origin is the desire of our Divine Source to express Itself in a way that will allow self-awareness and spiritual growth. Mars is the planetary vehicle for carrying the Divine Impulse to Incarnate on earth. He represents the principle of directed, purposeful energy. As Venus describes the physical substance of life, Mars describes its divine motivation.

When Mars is intercepted, the very idea of divine motivation is unknown or ignored. The entire environmental focus is in the physical and on its needs. If there is any thought of desire at all, we see it as something that conflicts with the need to conform, to please.

The Dynamics of Intercepted Mars

The Sun symbolizes the divine energy of spirit that creates and procreates life. As the offspring of that spirit, we inherit its traits. Humans have all the attributes of the Divine Person translated into a physical expression. Mars is the human equivalent of the Sun. He symbolizes radiant outreach as expressed through individuals. Son of his Father, he images energy for physical activity and creativity even as the Sun images spiritual energy for life. Mars symbolizes the *seed of divinity* in every human. He is most often called the planet of desire. DE-SIRE means "of the father." *Desires are the needs of spirit.*

Mars symbolizes our drive to *be like*, to *act like*, to *become like* our Divine Parent. By extension, he becomes the male or *son* image, even as the Sun expresses the male or Father ideal. As the sun symbolizes the *Spirit of God*, Mars symbolizes the *Human Spirit*. It is what Divine spirit *looks like* when channeled[1] into human form. It makes spirit visible.

When energy is concentrated, its motion slows. On Earth, the general energy field, the consciousness, is lower than the Source that created it. It must be. Like a child, it begins in an immature state and *grows up* to greater likeness with the *parent being*. As the child/son caries the genetics of the father, taking form in the mother's womb, so Spirit takes form in the Earth environment. All living beings are *born*, grow into physical maturity, then social maturity, then spiritual maturity, then. ... When they stop growing in some way, they begin to die.

Earlier psychic observers, noticing that the vibratory level *falls* when spirits incarnate, misinterpreted this as a negative and named the Earth experience a punishment. Not understanding that entities could or would *lower themselves* in such a way voluntarily, or that it could be a valuable experience, they condemned the entire Earth experience. Because they did not understand the nature of life and consciousness, they taught *spiritual seekers* that their only option was to lose consciousness. Their doctrine says that the only way to eternal life is to die and leave Earth. Since then Earthlings have tried to escape the planet.

Such beliefs have misdirected energy intended for discovery of Self, of Divinity, and of our relationship to it, into fight and flight. As a species, adrenal exhaustion threatens. Is it any wonder that diseases of energy depletion are becoming more common? If we do not learn to read and heed the warnings given by our bodies, the Earth Experiment must end and Source will be diminished by the very beings intended to expand it. Consequently, beings of higher evolutionary levels have *stepped their vibrations down temporarily*, to become incarnate on earth. It is our task to show the possibilities inherent in reaching for the greater life and higher consciousness that every person wants—even when they are afraid to know it, admit it, or try it.

---

[1] By the Moon/Soul.

Most humans have been so heavily programmed toward Eastern doctrines of *desirelessness* and/or western abhorrence for our *animal heritage*, that our survival instincts, of spirit and body, have been perverted. When Mars is intercepted, these perversions are taken as *fact*, as absolute reality, and that locks energy inside where it accumulates like steam in a boiler.

Intercepted Mars must refer to an exceptional knowledge of energy source and usage. If these beings could not survive on very little energy, they would not survive at all. The placement points to an energy-efficient body capable of functioning against its own creative consciousness. However, the body will feel like it is in imminent danger of starvation because the surrounding general consciousness will teach it so. Natives constantly *hunger* for something. When it originates in infancy, the feeling may translate to *thirst*[1]. Alcoholism may result. Food addiction is also common. When the will is strong, this hunger translates into other forms or activities. An apparent food addiction may have its roots in the need to assure a constant supply for an energy starved body. A compulsion to *people-please* may be rooted in the need to get others to meet our needs. At best, this hunger becomes a hunger for a more permanent satisfaction and drives us to seek enlightenment.

We have learned that energy is for *doing*, so when we feel energy, we *do* something, sometimes purposefully, sometimes not. With the intercepted Mars there may not be much *doing* going on. Excessive frustration of desire, at an early age, leads to depression, manifesting as fatigue. Natives suffer from *inertia*, not having what it takes to get started. Another version has *engines* racing all the time but they seem to be *out of gear*, and *spinning their wheels*. Darting from one thing to another, some people lack sufficient concentration to channel energy in a directed way for very long. Notice the *hypo- or hyper-active*, and *Attention Deficit Disorder*[2] victims.

Not knowing what kind or how much energy you have can cause an energy imbalance between the physical-emotional areas and the spiritual-mental areas. Natives have been taught to apply too much effort in some parts of life, while taking other areas completely for granted. Pairing interceptions of Moon and Mars is common. In such cases, the numbing of Lunar feelings forces Mercury's perceptive function into overdrive. If you cannot feel threat or pain or any other feeling, you must develop hyper-vigilance. Constantly watching, listening, for signals, you can never relax. This can use up vast quantities of energy, depleting supplies that might otherwise be used for experiencing or creating new things.

Intercepted Mars is almost as traumatic as intercepted Sun. With the solar interception, we cannot see our being or purpose. With Mars intercepted, we can probably see

---

[1]When you are hungry all the time, you can feed yourself or anesthetize the hunger pangs.
[2]Some are derived from Mars problems, as a problem in directing energy. Others are Mercury problems derived from perceptual difficulties.

them but cannot see how to accomplish them because we have divided physical energy from spiritual energy. The *survival instinct* compels us to focus on keeping the body alive, in spite of our opinion that it is not-good. An opinion is an idea and has energy. The energy of the opinion conflicts with the survival energy. This is like trying to run A.C. and D.C. through the same wire. Most carry around a mix of several versions of denied fear. We call this *wad* of undirected energy anger—or if sufficiently concentrated,[1] rage. Held hostage by fear of our *animal instincts*, the energy builds to an explosion. The explosion relieves the tension temporarily, but the energy soon begins to rebuild, predicting a new explosion.

Alternatively, it *shorts out*, overheating the body in a fever and/or high blood pressure. After years of this, some people have strokes as the life energy breaks out of its confines. Another variation simply grounds it back into the physical system, producing excessive weight, various types of growths, and/or deposits.

Understanding Its Effects

When Mars is intercepted, survival and/or self-realization become a life imperative. Only when survival is assured, is there time to consider anything beyond physical needs. Only when we know who/what we are, can we discover what is of value to our lives, and from that, what we want. In a civilized world, physical survival should be assured, but sometimes is not. For the general population, today's world contains far more threats to *spiritual survival* than to physical survival.

When Mars is intercepted, survival tools may be limited. When we reach adulthood with any part of being (any planet) intercepted, our physical survival is assured. On some level we know that so we *take it for granted*. Still, others may disagree with and/or challenge our survival abilities. Thus, the interception of Mars often shows that our early life taught us to fear annihilation of body or identity. We then channel all our desire energy into courage, the courage to defend our lives and our identities. Against all odds we struggle to be the unique individual we were born to be.

With Mars intercepted, often we must escape the environment of our childhood because it holds us like a prison. Then Jupiter must become the runaway, spending all its energy to keep us free to live and become what we were born to be. Only when Jupiter has freed us of all our *owners, controllers, enemies, parasites,* and other inhibiting relationships, can it fully manifest its inherent wisdom. Until that time it will be fully engaged in the problems of physical and/or spiritual survival.

When Mars is intercepted, Saturn must devote himself to protecting us from environmental threats. The result is that many of our restrictions are self-created. The very walls we hide behind become the boundaries on our existence, and even Uranus cannot take

---

[1]Look for a Pluto complication.

them down. This limits the Uranian function to that of adaptation, as we accommodate our lives to survive without hope of ever getting what we most desire.

Then it may be that Neptune brings her greatest gifts. Because the secret truth of intercepted Mars is absolute survival, from time to time we will forget to maintain our protection. Little by little those solid Saturn defenses begin to *melt* and a few Uranian surprises slip into our lives. Little by little, we discover that the seeming threats were mere illusion, no more solid than our belief made them. When we have faith in our Divine Desirability, Mars is finally free to reach for all that spirit needs to manifest its true purpose and mission in life.

Then, at last, the energy stored in the deep recesses of Pluto's realm will begin to activate, creating all that we have ever wanted. The desires of spirit will be created, powerfully, and our lives will begin to reveal our hidden magician.

The Effects on Aries and the First House

The Aries areas of a chart are like dormant (unpollinated) seeds or unfertilized eggs. Full of potential, they await quickening by the planet Mars. Aries is the divine seed of creation, awaiting fertilization by Mars. As sperm quickens ova, so Mars quickens Aries.

Aries is the possibility and the yearning of pre-existent spirit for life. It is the place where spirit awaits the touch of desire that makes it human, makes it live and grow and become. It is the field of incarnation, the urge to emerge into visibility.

Aries is the potential to be and Mars activates that potential from its desire to live. The touch of desire energy sets it in motion, allowing it to emerge from the soil, from the shell, from the womb.[1] Mars is like an electric charge, shocking Aries into motion, into action, into life. Here is where the future of all life is conceived.

The first house is where self-awareness begins as we create a mental image of whom and what we are. It begins with our reception into the lives of our parents. If we were wanted by the adults who surrounded our birth and infancy, we will develop a positive self-image. If we were not-wanted, we will develop a negative self-image.

Self-image is created from the names we are called, the descriptive words applied to us. It is not the true Self but is our idea of what that self looks like when viewed in the mirror of other people's eyes. If others tell us, "You are pretty, smart, good." or if they say that we are "homely, dumb, bad," we believe them. After that, when asked to describe ourselves we use these words. And when we think about ourselves, we think these words. They become our self-image.

When Mars in intercepted, the very question of whether the parents did or did not desire this child does not come up. Here the birth of the child was *taken for granted* as a nat-

---

[1] In Cancer or the fourth.

ural occurrence, not much more important than other events in the lives of these adults. We do not know whether or not we were wanted. Sometimes it seems we are simply not important enough for consideration. If we have a self-image at all, it is as *one of the Jones children*, or as *Jack's little brother, Jill's big sister.*

The Effects on Scorpio and the Eighth House

I do not consider Mars a ruler of Scorpio or the eighth house except as Mars/desires and Venus/values combine to produce Pluto's creative power. However, recognizing that some people still use Mars in these areas, this chapter has the necessary links for doing so.

The Scorpio areas of the chart are *fields of transformation*. They are places for the conversion of matter to energy, or energy to matter. Here energy is condensed to create form and/or released from form. The Scorpio areas of the chart are also *fields of generation*. Here, Mars' desire combines with Venus' values to create new life. While in Aries the survival issue is very personal (my life), in Scorpio it is social (the survival of humanity) and generational (children as the eternality of the parents).

If the energy of Scorpio is Martian at all, it is from the fact that in any conversion or transformation from one state to another, energy is released. With Mars intercepted that energy is often *free-floating*, without direction or goal, because we do not know what we want, or even that we want. Passion is concentrated emotion. With Mars intercepted, if passion exists at all, it must go into some other feeling, making one *powerfully needy* or *passionately self-less*, etc.

Without desire, sexual passion is buried, smothered, or simply invisible. Traditionally, this has been particularly difficult for males, because without Mars' male self-image, there is no motivation for heterosexual relationships. Hopefully, this marker is beginning to be recognized as wholeness, a state of spiritual evolution that is complete in itself. At such a level we are neither and both male and female, without the need of any strong sex drive. At this point Scorpio is fully converted to Pluto's rulership.

The eighth house is taboo for the child, intended for transformation to become adult assets. Often this produces the erratic energies of teen-age angst. Since adulthood is often recognized only in the context of marriage and children, these adult assets are frequently understood as marital or joint assets. They are then the result of joint-desires which intensifies energy for creation. Probably the only real connection to Mars' desires is that, not allowed the contents of its eighth house, the child chooses not to want them. There is, after all, no point in wanting what you cannot have.

The Appearance

Intercepted Mars must express through Venus. Without the necessary vitality or desire to reach for the desires of spirit, all desire must be channeled through the body as physical values. The Venus dynamic is that of attraction/magnetics. With Mars intercepted, its electrical energy must be converted to magnetism, producing an electromagnetic field. While the process is slower, it will attract those things which support our physical existence—our physical desires. By extension, that will support the eventual recovery of Mars. Until then, spiritual desires will be withheld or delayed.

Because Mars doubles as the *male image* in the chart, intercepting it is particularly difficult for males. Intercepted Mars can refer to a missing male role model. It can also take the form of a man who is *larger than life*. Uncertain of their own masculinity, some male role models may over-dramatizes their idea of male behavior.

Often natives were female dominated and/or fatherless. The assertive/aggressive parts of their personality have been forced inward, and intensified to the explosion point. When aggression is considered the predominant trait in definitions of masculinity, and the male image is constructed from ideas rather than experience, it can produce a *raw* or *animalistic* version of maleness. Intercepted Mars natives can recoil in abhorrence to the male image presented. They equate not wanting to be like their father (and perhaps the other men in Mom's life) to not wanting to be male.

Natives must then construct their own male image, as their fathers did, or take on one defined or explained by the women in their childhood, who may be man-haters. Many natives simply learn to hate maleness. Notice how hating maleness would affect the first-house self-image.

This background can lead to over-bonding with the mother, usually resulting in an inability to get far from her and/or from the original home. Alternatively, it can produce the overly macho male hiding a fear of inadequacy. Behavior ranges from the gigolo to the transsexual to the monk. The issues of sexuality are more role issues than truly sexual ones.

Adult male natives often have marriages which show too much or too little cohesion in a society that expects heterosexual unions to be co-dependant. The *spiritual effect* of this very difficult placement may force males to function more through their inner female. It takes the emphasis off ambition and drive, sometimes permitting the development of great psychic abilities. Consequently the women who marry them are more their mothers or husbands than they are traditional wives.

Others are offered the opportunity to prove the functionality or the *morality* of living in and through a variety of female roles. These might use their abilities to become secretaries, beauticians, artists, or even house-husbands and caretakers of children. At worst it self-destructs from frustration. At best it moves life to a greater integration of the male and female halves of the human psyche.

Frequently, intercepted Mars appears to be inherited. Some males are sons of repressed homosexuals, living in fear of female castration. The common belief that homosexuality results from psychological injury pervades their lives with fear around sexual issues. Others have grown up with a super-macho male who is fighting his own inner female. He may or may not have homosexual tendencies but he is homophobic and lives in fear of them. In these people fear may convert to anger because they cannot acknowledge it. Most are filled with barely suppressed rage which pervades the atmosphere. They do not always batter their families. Some vent their rage on objects or animals, but the threat of it hangs in the air continually. Alternatively, they become sex addicts and seducers who always have one or more mistresses in their lives.

For females, intercepted Mars can produce a generally poor opinion of men. Again, a dysfunctional male model during childhood is taken to be the correct one. Mother has usually had a great deal to say about *men*, which really only applies to the ones she has known. This can be a multi-generational thing. Mother's experience of her father has shaped her choice of mates, and her own father-experience is passed on to the daughter. If Mother has more than one husband, she usually goes from one version of her father to another, *proving* her thesis that men are *no-good, useless, stupid, simpleminded, uncontrollable or easily controlled,* etc. As a result, the daughter's early marriages may validate this learned opinion of men.

However, unlike her sisters with negative experience of males, the intercepted Mars native will usually not be convinced that all men are like this. She may be convinced that none are, but her early programming will betray her by attracting one who is entirely different from what she believed him to be. Often this forces her to develop her own inner male. This becomes a real impulse to spiritual growth. Like her brothers, she has the opportunity to help in raising the consciousness of inner union.

The Reality

Any being who can support a physical body and life without access to the spiritual impulse, cause, or meaning of life must have amazingly strong *survival instincts*. With desire numbed, need must substitute. Anything we want, we must learn to need. We create our lives around that theme, building a life structure that substitutes a physical need for an unknown or unacknowledged spiritual desire/need.

The strongest survival instincts are always at the beginning of any life cycle. The seed being must have the most drive so that it can emerge from the *darkness* of invisibility into the light of visibility. Intercepted Mars is always a new type of woman/man. The new is the undivided, the unit, the one. She or he is a direct image of the original One Spirit which is the source of life. She or he is, then, not clearly divided in gender because, in evolutionary terms, she or he comes before the conscious division or after that division has begun to lose consciousness. Technically such beings are asexual, being neither and both male and female. *Gender qualities* are undivided and/or have been reunited into complete unity.

Difficulties in expressing the surface masculine or feminine appearance are entirely derived from the ideas of maleness and femaleness in the general consciousness. When religious dogma has reinforced these, they are very powerful. The resistance to being sexless or genderless is powered by definitions which attach evil to what is different. Religious stasis threatens life. It is particularly threatening to intercepted Mars. Again, the desire to live must be incredibly strong if they are to live long enough to reach adulthood.

All interceptions must come to accept their differences as spiritual gifts meant for the evolution of the human species into its spiritual aspects. For intercepted Mars, this is critical. She or he must accept the spiritual truth that gender is simply a physical expression of Spirit, designed for producing life. Its two components must always be a desire and a form, a motive and a structure to make it visible. Without that Divine Martian Spirit, humanity is just another animal. With it, we are Divine offspring. Because of this we are impersonally desirable, meaning that while individuals may not like us, humanity-as-a-whole needs us. Because it does, it must and will support us, *when and as much as we understand that it must*. We can only be fully accepted as we accept ourselves, finding ourselves worthy and therefore desirable.

We are what we are because we are seeding the next generation of beingness. Models for spiritual (hu)manhood, we are the prototypes of what evolving humanity will become. We are seed beings in the finest and clearest sense. The recognition of our value to LIFE, makes us highly magnetic, drawing to us all that we need or want to make our lives and our roles in life complete.

Perhaps the greatest gift of intercepted[1] Mars is the realization of what, "I shall not want," means.[2] With Mars intercepted, all that we want is ours for the asking. The particular form that our spiritual mission takes, is the guarantee of its needs. Since its first need is a body, it also guarantees physical needs.

Although many have felt unwanted in the world of our early years, each is a vehicle for the Desires of Spirit. We are more spirit than form, the true *Sons of God*, in a new *seed* form. Representing a new impulse of Divinity, we are a new type of[3] Man, designed for the next age, even as the master Jesus was the prototype for this age. A larger population needs more such people, so they were seeded, broadcast across the world. Of all the Starseed/Possibility People, theirs is probably the most difficult task, for they fight the most resistance. These are beings of much courage and even more love. They need self-realization most of all. When they achieve it, they are to be honored above all.

---

[1]Or projected (7th house) Mars.
[2]From Psalm 23.
[3]Whether male or female. The masculine words are used in the generic sense.

Intercepted Venus

Intercepted Venus buries love, integrity, and sharing deep in memory under layers of conditioning. Like money in some lost or forgotten bank account, it may continue to collect interest, but it can neither support nor enhance the quality of our life. Sometimes this interception is mistaken for a lack of self-worth. Instead, it shows that our innate belief in the value of all life is so much a part of us that we do not question our worth. We know that we are valuable, but do not know how to express our value in ways that get approval.

The essence of the Venus principle is substance and its nature is magnetic. It manifests in the natural bond of attraction between objects of similar composition. Its principle is "like attracts like." With Venus intercepted, an assumption has been made that because the body does not disintegrate—because it is not sick or dying—its needs have been met. If it is alive, it is (automatically) loved.

This assumption then makes babies and children possessions of the parents, and possessions need less care than people do. Such infants will generally be fed and kept clean and presentable, but there will no recognition of any further needs. The child may be left alone for long periods, and its needs for touching and other sensory stimuli completely ignored.

The general consciousness holds a misperception that *blood* relationships are bound by love. In reality they are merely bound by societal rules. The only truly Venusian relationships are those consciously chosen by people who objectively value each other.

Value is a keyword here. *To be loved is to be valued for our existence, and for our uniqueness, as and for whom we are.* All too often, *need* is mistaken for or substitutes for love. Parents need children and children need parents. Need is neither a criterion for nor a guarantee of love. It can instead produce possessiveness, anger, resentment, a feeling of entrapment, and any number of other feelings in direct opposition to the true value of, or pleasure in, family relationships.

In the beginning, the *love* of parents for children is based on their value to the parents. That value is derived from their ability to provide a type of immortality for their parents. They may also provide a self-image—as a parent—for their parents. Sometimes children are surety for their mother's marriage, and indirectly, for her financial security. Some are proof of manhood for the father. If all goes well, the parents soon begin to love their child, *as an individual*, valuing its individual qualities.

However, with Venus intercepted, *love* stops there, remaining objective. Whatever *love* the child gets is derived from parental ownership. It is not directed to the child as Jack or Judy. There is no evidence of personal value in the early environment. Self-worth must then come from within.

The basis of children's love for parents is dependency. Human children are born helpless and must have one or more adults for survival. Of necessity, infants and young children value their parents as they value their own lives. Only as they mature can they begin to appreciate and love their parents as individuals, as people. Parents must prove their value to be truly loved. When they do not, children will still *need* them, but they will not represent a personal value to their offspring.

With Venus intercepted, we are expected to *know* that we are loved without any evidence or proof. Love is treated as a biological factor, automatically present in family relationships. It is as though the words *Mother* and *Father*—sometimes *brother, sister, grandparent, family*—are synonyms for love. Because of this it does not matter how these people treat us, we are expected to take it as an *article of faith* that we are loved and respond accordingly.

There is, then, an absence of real love in the environment. What the adults say love is, they do not practice. Still, they demand love from us. If we are at all conscious, it is natural for us to love them because we know that they are a survival value. On the other hand, our value to them is limited by their *need* for physical immortality and their ability to produce more children. They expect us to know what they want and need from us. Because we have no examples to learn from, people-pleasing becomes a lifestyle that uses far too much time and effort.

The Dynamics of Intercepted Venus

Intercepted Venus points to lack of integrity in our early childhood environment. In some way family unity was never present, or had been shattered.

Occasionally circumstances have torn the family apart. A parent/mother who dies very early, especially after a long illness, can cause major disruptions to the family integrity. Children may be *farmed out* to a variety of relatives, sometimes returning to find a family member permanently gone. In today's world, divorce and/or severe poverty might have similar effects, but usually enough love is present to offset the worst trauma.

For the occasional intercepted Venus child, life—as learned—is quite valueless. If it is to have value, they must create it. They may be so busy getting and keeping *things*, and sometimes people, that they have little time or energy with which to question their compulsive collecting of assets. In the worst cases they collect without discrimination, just to have more than anyone else. These are emotionally compulsive, subject to jealousy from the fear of losing everyone who loves them. In the worst cases, their fear dissolves the integrity of their acquired families, affecting yet another generation.

More often, the birth family is relatively unconscious, relating automatically, without thought, simply following a learned script. Nobody thinks much about love or needs. For them, human life is an automatic function, metaphysically not much different from any other animal behavior. When this is true, the *glue* that holds the family together is illusory. Few if any bonds occur within it, and it has no apparent reason for its initial or continued existence.

The intercepted Venus child in such a family will try to create bonds with other family members, and particularly between them. In a family where love has been *forgotten*, they take it as their task to remind others of what it feels like to be loved. With no *incoming love*, these devalued members of the family and of society struggle to fill great empty emotional voids in the lives of others, with their love. For many years this will deplete their ability to create those things which are most of value to their own lives. This becomes financially limiting.

The grace of intercepted Venus is that, devoid of all appreciation, these natives continue to value life itself. They know that their lives are of value to the world, but it may be many years before they give up their mission to make everyone else feel loved, and begin to magnetize their own desires. Only then do they discover *what they are good for*. Only then can they create the substance necessary to fulfill their true purpose and mission.

Understanding Its Effects

With Venus intercepted, the search for things and persons of value becomes a life imperative. We have a feeling of hunger that we cannot satisfy in the initial environment. This comes from a lack of good quality attention. Most natives have survived on minimal and often *negative* attention. They learn to use criticism, condemnation, and even violation and violence to maintain body integrity. Many develop attractions for unsafe or undesirable conditions or persons because that is their only definition of attention. It becomes *valuable* by default from the lack of any other attention. As a result they often learn dysfunctional ways of relating. It is important for them to realize that they can love others from a distance. Often they need to put much more space in relationships—especially those of the *significant other* variety. Until they do, they will find their time, energy, and money disappearing, as though down a drain.

An unconscious Venus can seriously damage the function of other planets. Without Venus' magnetism, attracting our lunar needs is difficult. Values and needs are closely related. Lunar *needs* refer to the basic necessities of life. Venusian *values* refer to those things that add beauty and pleasure to our lives. Venus can only do its rightful work when we first recognize the *need* for life enhancements, for rewards for our efforts, for recognition of our personal value to life.

Our highest value is our own life. To maintain that life, its needs must be met. The capacity to meet our own needs must be a primary value. When values are unconscious, need-recognition is limited. Primary needs will automatically be supplied from our essential recognition of the value of life. Secondary needs often go unmet because we do not know what will enhance our individual life, purpose and goals. We will have enough food, clothing and shelter *for survival*. We may not have the best food for our system, or the kind of clothing or shelter that is appropriate to our public image.

The great lesson for intercepted Venus is that we must value our own lives sufficiently to put our own needs first. Until we learn this, we put the needs of everyone else ahead of our own. Having been sent to the *back of the line*, over and over in childhood, we have accepted that as our rightful place. A major part of the maturation process must be to claim and defend our right to a full life *with all the trimmings*.

Integration is required for the formation of Saturn boundaries. Without boundaries we cannot accurately judge spacial requirements of relationships. Others invade our space and when we offer to share they simply take what we offer and appropriate it as their own. In rare cases, individuals become the invaders, but not without severe psychological damage.

Together, Venus and Saturn play a major role in the creative process. Saturn outlines the new creation, creating a void. Venus then magnetizes substance to fill that void. When Venus is unconscious, its creative aspect is hindered. It does not *fill-in* these creative voids well, leaving them to collapse in upon themselves. Sometimes nothing is created. Other times, what is created is significantly different from or less than what was outlined.

Without conscious recognition of what is of value to us, our Mars energy is poured into the collection of things that have no real relevance to our lives. Our true desires are *needs of the spirit*. If we are out of touch with our *spiritual values*/Venus, our desire energy will be derailed into *wasted effort* as we struggle to get what we think that we *should want*. We may not always succeed. When we do, it does not satisfy and our spirit remains hungry. In time we may stop reaching at all, settling for whatever *crumbs* fall from life's table.

Mars is energy and must go somewhere. With Venus intercepted, Mars' energy and out-reach often go into charitable pursuits. The native may seem to be desire-less. But true desirelessness can only be achieved when the creative consciousness has become fully mastered and automatic. When one has all that one could want, there is nothing left to desire.

Until then, intercepted Venus holds us at a level where Uranus and Pluto are ineffective and Neptune seems to dissolve all the changes we make or control we acquire.

The Effect on Taurus and the Second House

The Taurus areas of a chart are where self-worth needs expression. They are where we demonstrate *what we are good for*. It is where our most valuable personal qualities, aptitudes and talents are intended to express.

With Venus intercepted, the Taurus areas lack integrity and come apart. Here, all efforts to build something of value end in defeat, as structure after structure collapses from lack of a proper evaluation. Value recognition is the *glue* that holds form together.

The second house initially contains our conditioning about what we do have, or should have, as proof of the value of our lives. It can also be regarded as *gifts*—what we may have but not deserve. With Venus intercepted we do not recognize the value of the contents of our second house because we have not claimed them as our own or because we do not feel worthy of them.

With Venus intercepted during our early years, we have no *recognized value* because our most important personal assets go unseen or are mislabeled as liabilities or deficiencies. The second house then becomes what we *should have* but do not. Most of all, appreciation and payment are limited, until the interception opens, revealing the true value of our personal assets.[1] Metaphorically, our *goods* only become valuable to others some years after our birth. We may have a great deal stockpiled, but they cannot be converted into money, or other tradeable goods.

The Effects on Libra and the Seventh House

The Libra area of our chart is intended to reflect our Spirit/Sun/Identity. Here we are in partnership with the Divine. Here we become the *medium, channel, image/reflection* for Divine Spirit, which is the energy, power, motivation of our lives. "Made in the Image of God/dess," we are intended to *image* divinity in this house, distributing the *gifts of the spirit*.

However, with Venus intercepted, we have not learned to receive, only to give. We can only give what we know that we have. Here the connection to Source is damaged. We remain unaware of our *spiritual bank account,* so we do not draw upon it to replenish

---

[1]Either the interception opens or Venus (secondary) progresses out of it.

ourselves. Consequently, each offer to *share* becomes a *gift* that further depletes our funds of time, energy and/or money. Without Venus, we give a great deal but have almost no experience of sharing, because no receiving occurs. When we offer to share with another, that person takes what we offer as their own, leaving us with nothing.

The house of Libra is designed for sharing, cooperation and valuable conversation. Under the rulership of Venus it refers to shared values as the basis for relationship. When Venus is intercepted, it is difficult to maintain the correct space in the house of Libra because values are unequal. We do not know how close we can get to others without violating their boundaries. Neither do we know when to say no, so we permit others to violate our boundaries. This throws the seventh house completely out of balance as our *partnerships* are co-dependant rather than inter-dependant. They are established on the basis of *neediness*—where one partner *needs* the other and the other *needs to be needed*. All of this is based on a traditional form of marriage in which the genders were unequally—or at least differently—valued.

The seventh house initially represents our conditioning about what/how we are-not. Often these judgments are gender-linked and usually they imply a judgement against us. We then grow up with the idea that wholeness requires a *partner* to provide these *missing pieces*. From this comes the practice of referring to another as our *other half*—or, worse still, our *better half.*

The seventh house is designed to be a reflection of the first house self-image. Like a mirror image, it reflects what we think of ourselves. It perverts the Venus principle of "like attracts like." Instead, it insists that "opposites attract." The result is attractions based on perceived lacks in our self-image. When we look to another to complete us, we are forever doomed to failed relationships.

Successful relationships are about sharing. Sharing can only be done by equals-in-value. When Venus is intercepted, we cannot know our true value. Neither can we know our relative value. We have no means of recognizing our equals. Often we spend much time and energy in the attempt to love another into manifestation of their potential. Ultimately we are trying to prove our worth to others so that we can feel worthy to take our rightful place in society.[1]

Until a new ruler is found for Libra, an important task for Venus is to integrate the horizon (Ascendant-Descendant). Here we find all the conditioning about what we are/first house and what were are not/seventh house. This is a misuse of logic, which assumes that everything in life is either *good* or *not-good*. Some things are *good to be* and some are *not good to be*. Our self-image is built on our share of these *good* and *not-good* elements—*as perceived by the adults in our early childhood.*[2] But, the whole

---

[1]Our relationship to society is also a seventh house function.

[2]Virtually all conditioning is set by age seven, most by age three.

chart belongs to us. Some elements are dominant and visible, others are recessive and not visible, often unconscious. These usually get projected on other people, especially *significant others*.

We have the option to claim the entire chart. That is the goal of self-realization. Without integration the body and/or the self-image may disintegrate. Our life may be so disorganized as to accomplish little because we do not have the necessary boundaries to provide direction and concentration. The key to this integration lies in Venus, Taurus, and the second house, which must become conscious before we can claim the contents of our seventh house.

The Appearance

Intercepted Venus is forced to function through Mars or Pluto. When it functions through Mars, the body is held in visibility through the desire to live, generally called the *survival* instinct. This takes a high level of creativity, especially in a world where many are taught that having what we need is acceptable, but what we want is not. A major part of the rebirth factor will be the realization of the value that desire holds in our lives. We literally survive *because we want to*, not because any other in our earliest environment valued us sufficiently to nurture and/or protect us.

The ability to survive on desire alone shows an amazingly high degree of self-worth. The only things we are ever willing to spend that much effort to preserve are things we find valuable. Consequently, at some point we may be confronted with a situation in which we discover how much we really want to live.

Lacking consciousness of our innate attractiveness, we use our Mars outreach to seek love, to grab for it, to take what we need from the environment. We must become assertive (according to Mars' sign) or live alone and in poverty.

With Venus intercepted, the childhood has often had too much *discipline* and/or blame. More accurately, many were abused by adults who demanded or took things from their children because they felt inadequate in adult relationships. Abused children learn to fear attention, creating a double-bind between the need for attention and the fear of abuse.

When Venus must function through Pluto, some type of sexual abuse is common. Here, Venus love is forced to express through Pluto passion. In such cases the child has been expected to meet the sexual needs of an adult. Cooperation was coerced *in the name of love* and usually secrecy was compelled *in the name of love and/or safety*. These children were told that the secrecy was necessary to prevent hurt to someone or to prevent loss of love by someone. Either way, they learned that sexual passion is synonymous with love. The fact that the children had no choice in the matter further confused them. An adult always has power over the child—for a while. If the sexual abuse continues, the

Consciousness and Commitment

As the population increases, cooperation produces society. As society evolves, we develop more efficient methods of survival that free time for education and thought. When this happens, consciousness speeds up, producing more time-freeing technology, and the pace moves more rapidly.

At some point along the upward spiral, individual consciousness begins to vary a great deal more than it originally did, by necessity. The alternative would be to have non-human slaves to do certain tasks.

When humanity nears a *mutation point*, as when it nears the crossing from one age to the next, the variation is even wider and creating conscious, chosen bonds becomes even more problematical. When our beliefs about relationship exist at one level and our electrical fields are entirely different from the ones those beliefs were established for, commitments become difficult, even impossible to keep for long periods of time.

If we were wise, we would learn to do *renewable term* commitments. The problem is that to do so requires serious conversation and thought about division of property and sharing of responsibility for children. Most of us have been taught that these must be taken on faith, without question or analysis. To do otherwise is considered unloving. But is it?

child may eventually realize that the secret gives him/her power over the abuser. Then love becomes synonymous with control. Much of this is rooted in an obsolete definition of relationship and of Libra. It may be that the answer lies in a new rulership for Libra. Until then, some understanding of underlying principles may contribute self-awareness.

In relationships, a version of the magnetic principle holds society together. However, this is not the basic, *natural* magnetic principle. It is Venus applied in electro-magnetics producing something more like gravity. Here the *spin*, the activity of thought begins to speed up the natural atomic motion within the human form. In older esoteric texts, this has been called a raising of *vibration*. The modern phrase is *raising consciousness*.

Different levels of awareness in people, produce energy fields that are different in nature, volume, and pressure. In Libra, consciousness begins to *outweigh* structure in the Venus equation. Like thought now attracts like thought. Like belief attracts like belief—whether or not these are consciously held. The attractive force now functions through our conscious self-worth. What we think that we are worth attracts another with a matching personal evaluation.

In this society we often learn that anything outside the norm is lower in value. As a result, attractions may occur between people with fewer than normal abilities and those with more than normal abilities. The balance created is derived from the fact that your assets will offset my liabilities and we can then merge into the social norm.[1]

Observation of this has created an artificial corollary: "opposites attract." All the Possibility People are subject to these attractions, but intercepted Venus and/or Libra is probably most susceptible. They, quite literally, spend much time and effort trying to fill *black holes of hatred* with their love.

Channeling Venus through Pluto, we believe in the Power of Love—to transform anyone, anything. We struggle to fill the environment with our love so that none will go unloved. Because we cannot recognize the sensation of being loved, we pour this love from our own reservoirs, with no consciousness of being replenished, and it weakens us. Believing that evil behavior is a reaction to feeling unloved, we offer ourselves as victim to those who value power more than life. One of our life lessons is to discover that bonding/chemistry and love are different. Sometimes they are opposites. When love bonds with hatred life always suffers in quantity or quality.

For a few who come from the most severely disintegrated families, the only value held, the only conscious asset owned, is power—the power to control. These are emotional blackmailers. They can be dangerous, especially to those who love them. They take and use other people's love, as a control over them, enslaving them by the very power of their love. Most are adept at seduction, having an almost hypnotic control over others. They alternate *loving behavior* with acts of hatred skillfully, keeping their victims off balance, feeling confused and/or guilty whenever they wonder about the true nature of this *love*. Most suffer from paranoia and many are sociopathic. These are the takers of the world, and they never have enough to feel satisfied. Their hunger sometimes leads to antisocial behavior. Some run afoul the law and confrontations with death are common in this group.

Physically, intercepted Venus can produce anemia, low blood pressure, or low blood sugar culminating in diabetes. At its worst, it can produce AIDS, when the ego programmed *need to give* has overwhelmed the survival instinct.

The Application

The problem is not that we have been considered worthless, although sometimes that was true. Instead it was derived from the fact that the idea of personal value went unrecognized during the formative years. Our initial caretakers may have valued us because we were children, or because they *owned* us, but they did not value us in any personal way. Whatever was going on, all our magnetic energies were required simply to *hang on*,

---

[1]Remember that an interception can represent a regression as well as a progression. It marks anyone outside the *consciousness norm*, so it makes positive interceptions particularly vulnerable to their opposite numbers.

to stay in body and visible on earth. We were, quite literally, in danger of disappearing from lack of personal appreciation and attention. Almost anyone else would have died. We did not, and that should tell us something about our abilities to magnetize our needs—even from the invisible realm.

This does not mean that we were entirely unloved or unwanted. It does mean that, for whatever reason, we did not get the care and attention to our needs, considered necessary for normal development. Those whom we depended on for these things were too ill, too distracted, too busy surviving, or simply not present. Something intervened and we were left to keep body and soul together by sheer force of will or volume of energy. Some invisible power, derived from our value to life, kept us alive and met our survival needs.

Maybe we learned to teleport the bottles no one brought. Maybe an angel brought them to us, or a discarnate grandmother reminded someone to feed us. By whatever extraordinary means, we did survive major crisis during our earliest years and that should tell us something about our value to LIFE.

On another level, intercepted Venus refers to the ability to magnetize substance from other dimensions of time or space, to create the necessities of life. If we can do it to fulfill need, we can also do it to fulfill desire. When we do it consciously, we have control of our personal circumstances as far as we own, love, and value our desires[1] and/or our personal power. If we meet our own needs first, we will always have goods to share. When we own our talents, we will have personal assets to invest in others, in society, in LIFE.

Most of us go through periods of poverty and/or marital *failure*.[2] After we reach adulthood it becomes necessary to accept the fact that we can, and have always, met our own needs. Without this recognition, we continue to function at survival levels. We must *remember* or notice our ability to manipulate energy into matter to produce products that meet our needs. Most have almost no experience in anything beyond simple survival and it takes time to find a personally appropriate method of getting money and other assets.

Marital failures are derived from a cluster of beliefs common in the general consciousness. Usually we feel the *need* for another—if only so that we will be seen because we have an emotional *habit* of reaching out for attention. Traditionally, all women and most men *needed* to marry to achieve adult status in society. In addition, most have learned to base relationships on physical attraction. Finding that, we try to build some kind of cooperative structure over it.

This rarely works because the natural process has been reversed. Passion is intensity. Intense love equals passion, but passion does not require love. It may refer to intense need, anger,[3] sorrow, joy, communication—intense anything. Power is derived from an

---

[1]Because de-sires are the expression of spiritual needs.
[2]Legalized or not.
[3]The probable source of rape

accumulation of energy. If that energy is regarded as good, it will produce good results. If we regard it as evil, it produces (the appearance of) evil results. The only absolute power is love. Intercepted Venus has an innate understanding of that, but we must learn to love/value our power.

Alternatively, Love is energy, especially as applied in electro-magnetics.[1] Here we refer to the pure love of life which activates human outreach. Love expressed as action is being channeled through Mars. Passive, or static love is being channeled through Pluto. The first draws us to others. The second draws them to us.

The Reality

With Venus intercepted, we have evolved to a point where we know that the ultimate morality, the ultimate value, is life. Physical form and the survival of it, is the basis of all other value in life. Before there can be growth in consciousness, before there can be evolution, before there can be good works, or charity, or wisdom or any other value, there must be a living structure or entity to experience it.

The second reality of intercepted Venus is that we understand our relationship to Source as an equal one in which we share the joy and the responsibility for the ongoing creation of life. Deity is the unconscious absolute called existence. Being perfect, whole, complete, it is not subject to decay. Neither can it grow, transform, and/or become until it divides into invisible spirit/cause and visible form/effect. We are the conscious, living, growing, changing, becoming facets of Divine Beingness. Source anchors us in form. We anchor it in time-timelessness-eternity.

Our bond with Source is irrevocable. It is the only truly permanent *marriage*, for neither partner can long remain without the other. An unchanging element created from the beginning and an ever changing element that continually evolves are required for the continuation of life. The formless essence of life changes not. It is our foundation and Source. Formal structures endowed with evolving consciousness provide its future. Together we are eternal life.

In these two aspects lie the true value of life in all its forms and formlessness. To value is to love and it is our love for life that holds it together—whether we recognize it or not. On some level, intercepted Venus always knows this. She or he may not have the words for it, it may be invisible in his/her environment, but still she or he knows, still s/he trusts in the goodness of life. Because s/he does, s/he continually seeks to add value to it. Even those who value no other cling desperately to their own physical form. These add value to life in a very original way. Every electrical system requires resistance. Those who give up on love, resorting to hatred for power, provide resistance against which others strug-

---

[1]Love is the *magnetics* in electro-magnetics. Energy can be a wave-in-motion or it can be stored in/as physical form.

gle, exercising the strength of their love until they rise in consciousness, becoming the saints and angels of this world. Everything in this world is good for something.

Meanwhile, most intercepted Venus natives become formal expressions of Divine Love on earth. We might call some *white magicians*. Others are those great beings, like the Master Jesus who attract many through the simple technique of identifying as Love Beings. Wherever they go, they infuse beauty, order, harmony, and structure, in form, in relationships. They are the peacemakers, who are listed among the blessed. Each is a blessing. Each is blessed. All that they need to tap into vast treasures *laid up in heaven* is the awareness of their very real and sacred value to LIFE.

Intercepted Pluto

Intercepted Pluto hides our personal power under layers of condemnation in our value system. This can make us seem powerless, with no control over our lives or our future. Literally it hides the entire invisible realm from view, assigning the *dark side* to evil. But this is error, for the dark is only a place where light has not yet shown. It refers to ignorance, not evil.

More than that, all procreation begins in the dark, of the soil, of the womb. The greatest metaphysical mystery of all, the secret buried in the esoteric traditions, is that humankind is not *merely* a created being. Although the visible form of us may be *created*, along with the world and all other visible life, the essence, the nature of us, is procreated directly from Divinity. When our Divine heritage and origin are hidden under layers of condemnation for the physical, earthly experience, we lack the power to escape the consensus reality.

Pluto holds rulership over the esoteric traditions, because they hold the most potent of the *secrets of power* and because they clearly show how powerful a secret can be. For thousands of years an elite few have known the metaphysical nature of reality and how to use it for good and for evil. Because it was a *two-edged sword*, because its power was neutral, we could evaluate only its use. Whether from wisdom or from fear, this group has held these secrets as private, personal possessions, behind an elaborate security system. The highest members of every hierarchy of priests has known and used these secrets. Meanwhile, they taught a doctrine that declared magical powers evil, not be touched on pain of hell-fire.[1]

---

[1] There may be a bit of truth in the symbology. Esoteric texts generally contain instructions for artificially

Over the centuries, consciousness in the general population has risen drastically. The dimensions of awareness in modern humanity are vastly greater than they were a few centuries ago. As consciousness rises, it becomes increasingly creative. In the beginning, humanity was given *dominion over this world*. By our power to *name* life, we could change its action and appearance. In the realm of values, this was most creative and most destructive. This is the *field* of Venus and Pluto, who have been designated to rule personal and impersonal values. These were split apart by the power elite when the priesthoods and monarchies were formed.

At that time, most gave the general population ownership of personal, physical, survival values. Moral and ethical standards were set up under the guise of religions, claiming impersonal values for the priesthood first, and the monarchies second. They carefully sorted the available knowledge about the nature of God and Humankind, choosing what *lower beings*—the general population—were fit to know and what they might not be taught. In such a way, power was reserved to the elite groups. For a long time, even education was withheld, on the grounds of maintaining control over the general populations. This control was nearly absolute until around the beginning of the Piscean age.

Although his work was a synthesis of ideas from others who had gone before, the Master Jesus translated the great metaphysical ideas into the common language. The essence of his message was that we are Divine Offspring of our Creator. We inherit, not merely its property, but also its *genetics*. We have like powers and are intended to mature into a level of awareness where we can use them with intention.

The difficulty of intercepted Pluto is that these natives were born into a world, still under the control of those who believed that the division between the Elite and the People must remain constant. In the environment of our early years, this belief was accepted as *absolute fact*. It was taken for granted, *everybody knew* that *mental/magical powers* were either nonexistent, evil, or lead to insanity. Following the traditions of the past, natives were conditioned to fear taking control of their own reality, and to doubt the effects of those instances when they spontaneously did so.

The Dynamics of Intercepted Pluto

Pluto represents our personal ability to transform energy to matter, and matter to energy. That is the ultimate power that we have, and it is seated in our *word*—meaning inherent in consciousness. Consciousness is the part of Original Being projected or invested in humanity. We are the conscious aspect of Spirit, having been *inbreathed with the breath of life*.

---

raising consciousness. These are described in terms of opening and energizing chakras. At this level, awareness and energy are one. If you suddenly and drastically expand awareness, the resulting increase in energy could generate considerable heat, even trigger an occasional spontaneous combustion.

Currently, our clearest definition of Spirit is Being. It is our unadorned and unexplained sense of existence, the simple I AM. Any extensions or explanations of this must come from the human experience in a body equipped with senses. As the Sun represents *divine power* expressed in my personal life, so Pluto represents *human power* expressed as my impersonal life, OR as the conscious offering of my services to the WHOLENESS that we commonly name God. We are the means of extending the creative activity that originated with the Divine Parent through Its offspring and genetic heirs.

To claim my power, is to claim my *genetic inheritance,* from my Original Parent. It is the acknowledgment that I have the potential to become omniscient—a seer, omnipresent—an astral traveler, and/or omnipotent—a creator/transformer—a magician. Invested in these descriptions of God, commonly taught in Christian churches are all the *psychic* talents. They are our heritage and an aspect of *spiritual maturation*, otherwise known as expanded awareness or rising consciousness.

Perhaps the major religions of earth were, initially, justified in discouraging the development of these abilities. Foolish indeed is the adult who gives a child matches and sticks of dynamite for toys. Still, humanity increasingly grows, achieving ever greater maturity. If we are to reach our potential[1], we must push past the dogma of our religions to the truth hidden in all the great scriptures of this world.

Ages have passed, and the Divine Offspring are no longer *little children*. The time has come for the esoteric traditions to give up their secrets. We must claim our heritage, our rights, our authority, and our power. It is time that we become co-creators with our Source, so that the original creation may grow, expand, change, evolve. Only in that pattern can life-as-we-know-it continue for eternity.

Some have called Pluto the *passageway* between the visible and invisible worlds. From this comes its connection with death. The redemption Pluto offers, is the realization that death is merely a conversion from one form to another. If ever we face a demon, it is here, for we confront the first calculation error made on earth: the idea of *original sin.* Interestingly enough, Pluto is a small planet, but extremely dense and hard to penetrate. So is the dogma that misinterpreted a *fall in vibration*, as a *fall in value*.

As the Sun and Leo rule our physical genetics, so Pluto and Scorpio rule our spiritual genetics. Pluto's placement shows our capacity to recognize and use the human inheritance of the divine qualities of omniscience, omnipresence, and omnipotence, to create and re-create our world. By the laws of consciousness, if we continue to name this power evil, to fear it, condemn it, or even ignore it, our world will, in time, be destroyed. By those same laws, it can exist, expanding its awareness and influence eternally. This is what those who speak of "lifting the Earth to the next dimension," mean by the phrase.

---

[1]Notice the root of *potential*. It is the same root as potent and omnipotence. Potential is the possibility of using power—for creation or destruction.

The Metaphysics of Love

Creation is by word. The creation is good. Humanity is given dominion over the Earth—our word holds creative power on Earth.

We think logically from a dual principle, as a means of developing consciousness. Consensus reality misuses choice and judgment due to a misunderstanding of duality. This brings condemnation to earth. To the initial goodness of life, humanity adds evil, by naming it so. If evil is to be overcome, the initial error/sin must be overcome. We must rename this World, calling it a good place, and revaluing human life as good experience, with a valuable purpose.

In condemnation and judgement, Venus/Love is then fallen *in vibration*. Grounded to Earth, it is grounded to error. On this error, Christian dogma has been built. All its potential for goodness is weakened by that basic flaw in its *foundation*. Almost half the power available to the *Divine offspring* called human, is being held hostage by our concept, our *word*, our belief in, evil.

We struggle to overcome evil. In the end, we must discover that it was only a formal construct built of errors in judgment. Satan may *look* solid, but he is only a thought form, created from the perceptual mistakes and misnaming of a youthful humanity still learning the nature and use of a personal consciousness.

Ultimately, Pluto symbolizes the power to generate or regenerate life. Most of its concepts have been hidden in the esoteric traditions, available only to those who sought diligently for them. The planet was unknown or invisible until early in the twentieth century. Interception symbolizes birth in an area where Pluto's principles remain undiscovered, out of fear or ignorance. The context of our early childhood has entirely ignored the possibility of a divine genetic heritage, considering personal power an evil to be avoided, even feared. Power and *magic* simply did not exist, or were *dead issues*.

Only time or relocation will resurrect our personal power, bringing it into the light of awareness. Until then it will function sporadically, as any unconscious ability will do. With the judgments on science and/or magic in place, they can only produce destructive action until the interception opens. Transits of Pluto usually remove something from our lives, *as though it had never been*. The divine intention is to open the *closed doors* which hide our spiritual talents, so that our ability to manipulate and control our personal reality can be revealed. Consequently, Pluto transits are often involved in opening intercepted areas of the chart, removing the hindering ego programing, as though it had never been. We experience this as *rebirth*. It is an opportunity to know the essential being which exists behind and within, both before and after, our physical self.

When Pluto is intercepted we often spend years with no clear understanding of the value of power. In our learned value system we have taken it for granted that all power belongs to authorized authority figures and that reaching for it is an unloving act. We were usually taught that all *magic* is evil, that denying our inherited abilities to use power is good, and loving behavior.

We can never bring Pluto into the light without a clear understanding of Divine, Impersonal Love. Pluto's power is the *power of naming* described in all the esoteric magical texts. The entire process of increasing awareness and consciousness raising is directed to discovering how the way that we *name* the structures and events of our life, and the value implied in that naming, determines our reality.

For thousands of years humanity has been in denial of that original error, preferring to think of it as a character flaw derived from their *animal nature*.

All that we have ever needed was a *change of mind*. The great difficulty was that with the development of religious doctrine, the error was held in place by *moral codes*. It became so deeply ingrained in the world consciousness that it was passed from mother to child in the bonding process. Only time and the development of science and technology could bypass this emotionally coded denial. Through them humanity was destined to rediscover its lost powers, from the context of life. When civilization freed more time for thought, the human mind began to *slip its conditioned bonds*. As it did, the monarchies and priesthoods of the world began to lose their hold.

With the birth of the great seed beings[1], near the beginning of the Piscean Age, the discovery of the trans-Saturnian[2] planets became probable. The recognition of an impersonal consciousness in humanity soon followed. As they did then, those beings carrying the *Mark of the High Calling*, symbolized by interceptions and Yods, are seeding the possibilities of human development during the Aquarian Age. Of them all, Pluto carries the greatest transformative power. Its purpose is to teach us the lesson of the butterfly, who lives one lifetime on earth, then *by its own nature*, is transformed into a beautiful creature of the sky.

Understanding its Effects

The effect of intercepted Pluto is like being born into a *caterpillar world*, entirely unconscious of the possibilities of personal evolution. To the adults in our early childhood, butterflies seemed like irresponsible beings, unconcerned with the difficulties of life on the ground. Many of these too-grounded beings hate butterflies and wish them ill, not realizing that they are looking at their own future. The distance from their world to butterflies seen against a sunlit or starry sky seems very far and unattainable. Their *scientists* deny them hope and their churches make belief in that possibility a *sin of pride. How dare they try to reach God? Surely this is sacrilege!*

---

[1]Such as Buddha, Lao Tsu, Kung Fu Tse, Socrates, Plato, and Jesus of Nazareth called Christ.

[2]Uranus, the great remodeler. Neptune, the great dissolver of obsolete form. Pluto, the great rebirther.

Every person whose chart is marked by interception, is intended to live the lesson of the butterfly. Intercepted Pluto lives it symbolically, impersonally, as an archetypal image. Lives of these beings graphically present an image of death and resurrection. How appropriate that since Pluto's discovery, the *science* of CPR has given professionals the ability to restart human hearts! Where Pluto is intercepted, this experience is often quite literal, but its significance is the life change that goes with it. If life does not change significantly, the symbol has failed and we may need to repeat it.[1] Literally, intercepted Pluto gives the power to start life again on a new foundation. It defines life by birth, death, and rebirth.

Pluto's most significant ability right now, is the power to escape our conditioning by changing our point of view. This is the *death of ego* taught by teachers in earlier times. Today we teach, not its death, but its transformation. A key goal of our teaching is the re-alignment of the ego structure with the identity structure. When this is done, we are empowered to *reach the stars*, and beyond. Intercepted Pluto's task is to do this in a rather public fashion, as an illustration of the use of personal power in our everyday lives. The intended result is to free us from the current consensus reality, and to set the formulation of the new dimensions of reality in motion. These have the power to affect the world for generations to come—sometimes directly, more often indirectly. Pluto's power is distinctly cumulative, multiplying exponentially over an extended period.

The Effect on Scorpio and the Eighth House

Intercepted Pluto leaves Scorpio under the rulership of Mars. It then becomes a place of frustrated desires because intercepting Pluto has robbed him of his creative powers. Without personal power, Scorpio can only manifest in sexuality and manipulation, often combining the two into sexual abuse. There are two primary forms of this. Some demand their *sexual rights* from unwilling partners. Other natives use seductive behavior and withholding of intercourse to control their partners. This may or may not be connected to the ancient notion that sexual energy should be conserved to increase personal power.

Natives rarely claim their *adult assets* from the eighth house. It remains a place that is largely taboo, creating financial difficulties within marital unions. Much money may go through the family budget, but it is often so poorly managed that property loss and even bankruptcy continually threaten.

---

[1] A man of our acquaintance, with Pluto opposite Mars intercepted, has been revived at least four times, resisting change each time. Recently he was given a heart transplant. We have no news since then. We note that, intercepting both planets is as critical a life and death situation as there can be. His beliefs are killing him, but his spirit keeps resurrecting him.

The Appearance

When Pluto is intercepted it is disconnected from Venus in the ego instructions. We learn that power and love are mutually exclusive principles. When we accept that as true, power must be vested in hatred and evil. Following logic from there, love becomes powerless and weak and logic takes us into dangerous territory. If we are to avoid having destruction overwhelm construction and anarchy overwhelm our social structures, we are compelled to *step back* and take a longer, wider, more inclusive view of life. We must begin with a cosmology which predates structured religion. If humanity is to be *saved*, if it is not to destroy itself, we must discover our true value in the structure of life.

Viewing Venus and Pluto as the two poles of a magnet is important. Put together one way, they attract. Reverse them and they repel. The opposite of integrity is an explosion. One side of the magnet holds life together. The other lets obsolete structures be destroyed and their essence invested in more productive uses. We cannot plant a garden without *tearing up some ground.* We cannot bake a cake without *breaking some eggs.* Physical life is impossible without some destruction. It also becomes impossible if clogged with over-construction. Like all else in life, construction and destruction must achieve a balance if life is to remain worthwhile.

The value of physical life is vested in our *genetic* relationship to the Creator of Life. If that Creator is Good Incarnate, we, as Its offspring, must also be essentially good. If we are at all rational or intelligent, it must also be intelligent. God and Humanity differ in two ways and one of these is illusion. We can see each other, but we cannot see God. We have senses that allow us to view life from different perspectives, and to learn from those perspectives. This gives us an illusion of time and space, which gradually expands our horizons until they disappear. As our level of awareness rises, our *vibration* rises and we draw closer to our Divine Origin—not in space or time, but—in consciousness. Our energy *speeds up.* We *disappear from* this world, simultaneously *appearing in* the next.[1]

As consciousness rises, we become more aware of how it acts to create life. Discovering our *inherited talents*, we achieve enlightenment. The potential to perform magic and miracles through the intentional manipulation of mind and matter is in our *genes.* The unconsciously used phrase "mind over matter" is far truer than most realize. From the beginning, the *Word* could create matter, and mold it into formal structures called worlds, or possessions, or dollars.

The principle of love/magnetics is critical in this process. Wherever we focus attention, vibration slows sufficiently to turn *pure* energy to matter. Matter is naturally mag-

---

[1]Certain esoteric writings have described a series of *heavens* each with a higher level of vibration, to be passed through. This may or may not be true. The principle holds true. We are visible to those with like *frequencies*, and invisible to those with unlike *frequencies.* Thus, as consciousness rises, we see new images, at first translucent and blurred, gradually appearing more solid. This is the origin of argument about the presence of ghosts, angels, aliens, etc. Each human sense has this potential for increasing its *bandwidth.*

netic/attractive, and will draw other *like matter* to it. However, the definition of it rests with consciousness. If we say that this is good matter, we imply that it has certain qualities which are, *in our opinion or experience*, personally valuable. When we mentally focus on something that we wish to avoid, that focus also establishes matter, and it attracts more *no-good* substance. If we have one *good* object or experience and another *no-good* object or experience, by our thought and belief, one may overcome the other. If we can discover the good in the *negative* factor, the positive factor may use its substance. Alternatively, the process can be reversed.

Pluto symbolizes our potential to reformulate anything, changing it from negative to positive, or from positive to negative. That is the basis of magic. In application, it can be proved at the levels of values and of awareness or visibility. The magnetic principle, applied with consciousness, can and has created and destroyed worlds. Even so, it can create or destroy your personal world because the Power is magnetic—neither good nor evil.

When Venus is intercepted, we are unaware of our ability to attract our good. When Pluto is intercepted, our innate resistance to *evil* is denied. Only when the interception holding these planets opens, can we discover the possibility of fusing all the power to one side. If we try to fuse it to the *wrong* side, it will be destructive to our life. If we fuse it correctly, Love and Power are merged as the Power of Love—which it initially was before we polarized it. We may then learn to Love our Power, understanding its potential for creative evolution. Each level of goodness will then be superseded by a greater good, as consciousness rises.

Personal power is a requirement for adult life on this world. Without it we have no control over anything and are the ultimate victims in life. For the intercepted Pluto native, simple survival has required all our personal power. From the beginning, these children have *battled evil forces*. They have been victims of the beliefs in their environments, and have consequently suffered illness or abuse. Many have insane and/or addicted adults surrounding their childhoods. This represents some threat to physical life, and more threats to the development of a personal consciousness that is adequate to deal with adult reality. In some way life has taught them to take evil for granted, and to go on *loving their enemies*.

The conflict comes from beliefs in the general consciousness that all parents, grandparents, etc. love these little ones. Small children must believe in a benevolent world at all cost. To believe otherwise destroys their will to live. When the surrounding adults are too *sick* to love, the child may believe that it is worthless or evil. They condemn themselves because their inability to hate—even to hate evil—compels them to believe that they are causing the hateful behavior being displayed by the adults in their young lives.

Serious over-bonding with a powerful, possessive mother is a common accompanying problem. A psychologically healthy mother will allow, even encourage, the separation necessary for maturation of her child. One who discourages maturation may pretend it is for love, but it is a life-limiting, life-destroying practice, rooted in hatred of her own life.

Under-bonding or intimate exposure to too many people too early in life, can produce similar effects, making learning of language skills exceptionally difficult. Natives must usually choose between the ability to speak well, and reading and writing skills. The fact that they learn any of these abilities at all, is a clear indication of a powerful consciousness. Without that asset, they would become autistic. In this world, the lack of good language skills, limits the power we have over our own lives. It is nearly impossible to function without the ability to read and write. If we cannot give meaning to our lives, or if we cannot express our ideas and thoughts, our lives become increasingly proscribed and powerless.

Probably more significant is the general belief that those who lack language skills also lack intelligence. In a world run on language and communication, this seriously damages self-worth. In worst case scenarios, it can lead to self-hatred, to hatred of life, to hatred of everyone. These are then labeled the criminally insane.

The Reality

At best this placement pushes natives past the realms of ordinary logic and communication, producing seers and telepaths. Pluto is, after all, the conversion principle. When it is intercepted, it forces us to find ways around the results produced by our childhood programming. If we cannot read our books in the ordinary way, we may, like Edgar Cayce, *sleep on them*, absorbing them in an alternative way. When we do not perceive or learn in the usual way, we must tap our *deep memories*[1], for the information necessary to live in this world. Many learn to reach entirely through the personal subconscious to the universal consciousness, and/or the Akashic records for information. We must then adapt it for use in practical ways if our lives are to function in any *normal* way. It is remarkable how often individuals with Pluto in primary or secondary interception do the *improbable,* even the *impossible.*

In so doing we learn to tap inspirational and intuitional levels for information as naturally as anyone else might use an encyclopedia or a library. A prime example is Einstein, who was so dyslexic that he could not tie shoes, but produced the most inspired mathematics seen in centuries. I know one intercepted Pluto native well. This man developed excellent skills as a trance channel and had access to vast quantities of knowledge. His letter-writing skills were so poor as to make the process nearly impossible. His spelling, handwriting, and grammatical skills function at around the second grade level. He was seriously handicapped in career areas, even while considered a guru by many.

---

[1]Probing deep in the subconscious, even entirely through the personal consciousness into the universal consciousness.

Because of these difficulties, which function like *shorts in their wiring*, intercepted Pluto individuals are forced to remember and develop their magical skills. Before they can do so they must get past the condemnation of such abilities that resides in their value system. They are required to take their abilities to use power and to manipulate reality out of the dark and bring them into the light. They need not *advertise*, and would be well advised to keep their own counsel. Those who can learn from them will notice the paradoxical appearance of lives that are often supplied in unusual ways. When those who cannot *learn* know more than those who have great educations, a question arises about where information really originates and who has access to it. These questions lead modern chelas to seek out these Plutonian gurus. We can learn much from them, just being in their presence.

Most of all, intercepted Pluto presents a living Principle of Transformation to the world. These are the reformulators of reality, whose lives are invested in empowering the future. They are here to lead the way into the next age, the next reality, by the power of the *Word*. The words they speak are often "Open sesame." Other times it is a simple "Let there be light."

Theirs is the hardest task. They are here to overcome the last hurdle, to open the way for a return to Paradise. Many do not make it for themselves, living lives of suffering, in the belief that they are experiencing some kind of Karmic justice. Like all intercepted charts, these represent beings who have long ago *graduated* from the Karmic wheel. They have stepped back in time, giving up much of their power, to show the means of, and the necessity for, developing personal power.

Their lives can be highly visible, and many benefit from knowing them, but living lives of struggle is common for them. Even so, at the end—and often not before—their essential goodness does overcome the evil that seems to seek them out. Many suffer long and pay a high price for their investment in the evolution of humanity. Still, behind all the pain, a childlike joy breaks out in their lives from time to time, clearly showing that life always overcomes death and good always overcomes evil.

There are only two real powers in life. One is Consciousness; the other is Love. When they are merged through the lives of Intercepted Pluto natives, we have the opportunity to see the glory and the power of our Divine Heritage, made manifest on earth. The great thing about this lifestyle is that natives clearly change the lives of many, even when the task seems hopeless and thankless. We feel certain that when the rewards are withheld in this world, they will be all the greater in the next.

As the years pass and we move into the next age, these beings will come into their own. Finally the world will *catch up with them* sufficiently to appreciate them. What is more important, it will advance sufficiently so that they can appreciate and value themselves. When they no longer condemn themselves, no other power will or can. Their magic was never *black*. It was merely an unknown factor, hidden in the darkness of ignorance. All it ever needed was its turn in the light.

Intercepted Chiron

The intercepted Chiron functions somewhat differently than that of other planets because it is new on the scene. Until its discovery in 1977, it was, in effect, always intercepted because it symbolizes a range of choice previously unknown to the general population. With the advent of Chiron and the rise in consciousness that it represents came the discovery of the principles behind the ability to do *magic* and *miracles*. During the following years, many people discovered the ability to channel information and communication from previously unknown levels of reality. This was followed by a new sense of personal power, as individuals learned to use attention creatively in changing their world. Still, for several generations, the acceptance of humanity's spiritual heritage would remain spotty among the general population. Where it is still not generally accepted, individuals who are intuitively gifted are often born with Chiron intercepted.

When Chiron is intercepted early in life, the entire idea of personal choice in our approach to life is buried under a confusing Neptunian fog of *irrational faith* in the form of religious dogma. Doctrines of *original sin* and *unending karma* have long been used to control spiritual growth in the masses. These have made life hard work. Sometimes it takes so much energy that we become ill from exhaustion-related causes (example: Chronic Fatigue Syndrome). Even when we do not become ill, we struggle for years under heavy loads of guilt and duty.

Wherever Chiron remains denied, Neptunian fog takes up residence. Fear may supercede a *faith* that seems not to work for us, regardless of our trust in it. The root cause is that we have been denied access to large areas of the human consciousness-structure and of the physical brain associated with it. Laden with *karmic burdens* and *loss of inno-*

cence, true spiritual growth is contained and controlled by those who usurp control in the name of their abusive, insane gods.

Consequently, our intelligence has been confined to the use of ten percent of our brains. Until quite recently, the entire right-brain was often denied as irrational, useless and/or evil. Many religions expected followers to accept certain tenants-of-faith without rational analysis, denying many choices on *moral* grounds. Meanwhile, science refused to accept anything which could not be handled with the physical senses, adding further denial.

For the general population, using more than a small portion of the brain was not a choice. The remainder was an unknown. It sometimes came up in dreams or art, but taking it seriously was routinely disallowed.

One of the more interesting things about Chiron is that it was not found outside the orbits of planets discovered earlier. Instead, its orbital path tracks from the Jupiter side of Saturn's path to the Uranus side. It has been there all along, awaiting notice.

Then, around the time of Chiron's discovery in 1977, the general population began to be exposed to the possibility of wider choices. We began to understand that we have both inner and outer senses, and finally, the creative consciousness began to emerge.[1] Even as adults began recovering suppressed abilities and talents, generations of the most aware and evolved beings the world had ever seen began to be born. Humanity was being *up-graded*.

The Dynamics of Intercepted Chiron

If Chiron were truly withheld, you could not choose what to wear or eat, or even whether you should get out of bed each day. You would never grow up, remaining dependant for your entire lifetime, much like those with severe developmental disabilities involving hampered motor skills.

Mercury, Chiron, Jupiter, and Neptune symbolize the components of our consciousness structure. Mercury gathers and processes data. Jupiter calculates conclusions from that data. The ease with which this can be done depends on the efficiency of our *filing system*. Chiron organizes files experientially. It takes the *data* that Mercury has entered into our memory files and adjusts it to fit our personal reality—literally making it our own. It is an information *handler*, setting up our personal and short-term memory filing system. Fully conscious, it can also interface with Neptune's *extended memory*.

Neptune is the place where apparently *lost* or *forgotten* information is stored—including that which originates with other incarnations and other persons. When dealing with

---

[1] Notice the changes in television programming. These now include not only angel and aliens, but witches and professional psychics.

Neptunian sub and super consciousness, Chiron becomes the *modem* or channel through which such information can be *selected*, remembered, and transmitted back through Mercury into verbal form, or used by Jupiter in some calculation or computation. In the highly evolved, it may also act as a *search engine*, reaching into that field called *Universal Consciousness.*

The interception of Chiron shows that this capacity is an unknown in the environment of your earliest years. You were taught that the consensus reality is all there is, that there are no other dimensions to reality and/or consciousness. Whatever you *remember* that does not fit with the current *party line* will be called unreal, a dream, or your imagination. This creates Soul Wounds, related to the way we *stuff ourselves* into the pattern of adult expectations.

When the memory of Soul Wounds is deeply buried and forgotten, as most pre-verbal experience is, life and Chiron will present us with similar circumstances in our adult lives, offering us a chance to heal them.

Pretending that our childhood was optimal, even perfect, never works. We are required to see our parents clearly, for what they were, allowing them to be as human as we are. Until we do, repeating difficulties in relationships, career, and sometimes health, insistently offer us the opportunity to complete the *unfinished business* of our childhood.

Repeating patterns of dysfunction are symbolic memories that come up for resolution. They force us to recognize that the parenting we received did not serve us well—at least in some areas. When we can allow ourselves to see and accept the fact of family dysfunction without bitterness or blame, we can free ourselves of its effects. When we were infants, our parents were gods. As adults, we must permit them their humanity!

Chiron is our personal data handler, capable of a wide range of file handling functions. When we expand our mental/perceptual connections to greater realities, Chiron becomes the *modem* through which Mercury can pull information from the impersonal areas of Neptune's memory, in the same way that we pull information through our internet connections. Chiron is quite adept at finding information in our *memory files*, and those files go back into prior lifetimes. However, with Chiron intercepted, it will be some time before we acquire the knowledge that this is true, or develop a method of memory retrieval for certain areas. Here is where divination techniques and (self) hypnosis become useful.

Chiron is rational to the extreme, based entirely on logic. It can only deal with what Mercury has given it. Like personal computers, which are its corollary symbols, Chiron demands that we follow specific routines and methods. Data entered incorrectly will not process, and may *lock up* the computer in frustration because it cannot do the work requested of it. When we *do everything right*—as instructed—and get the *wrong* results, we are being confronted with a Chiron issue. Some belief that we have accepted as fact is clogging up the system.

Chiron rules coordination. When we have a conflict between our inner senses and our outer ones, we say that we have a coordination handicap: dyslexia. Even with *normal* coordination, periodically, we need to reorganize our thinking, reordering our filing system for the tasks ahead. Routinely, life demands that we *check* the rules, or the manual, or our own experiential memories. Interception can prevent us from realizing the difference between *our ability to make the rules work for us* and *the ability of the rules to work for anyone.* This can make guilt and a feeling of imperfection major life hazzards to be overcome. When your interception opens, full awareness of the Chiron function will reveal your innocence, setting you free of guilt. Chiron can play the role of saving grace.

Chiron cannot generate information; it can only process it. Utterly pragmatic, Chiron governs process and method, working rules, and/or scientific law. Chiron is concerned only with availability and accessibility of data and has no capacity to judge that data on moral grounds. Its only criteria are: "Does it make sense? Does it work—efficiently or at all?" Until we retrieve Chiron, we may not ask these questions, and we desperately need to do so, for there are errors in our conditioned *working knowledge.*

Intercepted Chiron forces us to confront issues of rationality. How much of what we learned about dealing with life makes sense? If not, why not? How will we heal our wounded Souls? More than most, the intercepted Chiron must heal itself. To do so, we must analyze our belief systems for inconsistencies. Often, in the process, we reach entirely through the surface portion of consciousness into the Neptunian realm. For many, the manifest image of Chiron will be something like astrology, tarot, runes, or other *divination* techniques which can help us connect with our inner senses.

Chiron is the great facilitator, searching out the easiest and most efficient methods for dealing with the consensus reality. Because of its drive for efficiency, it can exceed its own original limits. Its interception leaves a void that gets our attention. We have to make Chiron conscious if we are to heal ourselves, and make our lives work. From there it is but a step further to become a healer of other wounded souls.

Most important, Chiron is about choice. The most important of these choices is the choice to grow, to become, to heal, to evolve. Like the army, Chiron offers the opportunity to *be all that you can be.* When it is intercepted, you have chosen life circumstances that will force you to make that choice.

Understanding its Effects

At its least conscious, Chiron rules *normal* developmental cycles such as puberty and menopause. When it is intercepted, normal developmental cycles may be disrupted, making maturation difficult. Look for the origin of this is in the early environment. While natives are still emotionally connected to the Mother, and before they learned to distinguish themselves from her, she may have lived by *following her feet*. For one reason or another, she seemed to have no choice in where, or how, or with whom she lived.

Alternatively, in rare instances, children are not given the opportunity to learn how to choose. Reaching adulthood, they are left to make whatever adjustments are necessary to permit them to survive in a choice-less state. It may be years before they notice that *making no choice* is a choice in itself.

The underlying purpose of making choices and adjustments is to permit us to coordinate and/or synchronize our physical and spiritual development. An inhibited Chiron can leave natives feeling *out of sync*. With Chiron intercepted, we often seem to be much older or much younger than our chronological age. Very often we are *too immature*, too dependant, in some areas, and *too mature*, too independent in others. The resulting feeling may be translated as an uneven flow of life with *too much help* at times and none at other times.

Worse, it teaches us to mistrust our perceptions, creating coordination disabilities like dyslexia. (Alternatively, such disabilities can be shown by difficulties around Mercury that cause us to doubt our capacity to see, hear, or sense correctly.) Chiron difficulties differ in that we doubt our capacity to use what we learn from our perceptive function (Mercury) in any rational way. Metaphorically, Mercury might represent an absence of information or an inability to absorb it. In the same way, Chiron might represent an inability to use or apply the available information. It would be too vague, or *slippery*, to grasp. To the client, it matters very little, because s/he learns to mistrust his or her senses either way. To the astrologer it may be very important because the peripheral effects of the two conditions vary. Mercury problems represent perceptual difficulties—a hearing or vision loss, for example. Chiron problems represent comprehension problems—you can see/hear/sense correctly, but have difficulty using the information presented by the senses. We may have unlimited information which seems useless to us because we cannot link it to experience in ways that allow us to move past it.

Effectively, intercepting Chiron forces us to use Neptune for making life transitions and adjustments. We are required to *tune in* the necessary information because we have no recent experience relative to what is ahead of us or what is expected of us. This can feel like we got into the wrong world. We are not merely strangers in our family, culture, or country, we are strangers on Earth! This is difficult enough, but when the native is highly evolved—and most people with interceptions are—his or her own creative consciousness can formulate further alienation. The more we identify w*ith our strangeness*, the more *estranged* we become. Consequently, it is important to realize that we are simply ahead of our time, and that we are designed that way to become living examples of new ways to handle life and its problems.

A side effect of this placement is that without Chiron's capacity for organizing thought, it can be difficult for Jupiter to calculate conclusions. The logical process is disrupted. When this happens the intuitive process must substitute, and we survive on our *instincts*. In a world biased toward logic, this is often criticized. That very criticism is illogical. Does it really make sense to spend time calculating a conclusion that you can simply *call up* from memory?

How do the critics of intuitively based individuals think that the information got into memory? The only reasonable answer is that at some time (in some past life) it was logically processed and *saved*.[1] Omitting Chiron-awareness from our lives leaves us with a limited view of human consciousness—one that does not recognize that we can *know* things that are not in the personal/immediate or short-term memory. Until you know that it is possible to remember such things, they are, for you, nonexistent. As your interception opens, Chiron will build a bridge which links the various levels within your consciousness-structure–effectively *plugging you* into your *personal internet*.

An interesting development of this condition is that natives sometimes go *through the subconscious* to the place where the memories of thought process are stored and begin to think logically. This is the real meaning of the Oureboreous symbol. Realistically, it is consciousness come full circle, beginning again from a much *higher* or *greater* base.

Intercepted Chiron can withhold our *right work*, and sometimes health information. Some natives may suffer from obscure metabolic diseases, simply because they have internalized the belief that somehow they *don't work right*. Finding the correct diet can bring rapid healing, particularly if combined with daily affirmations like, "Perfect body, perfect mind, perfect me."

Since Chiron is related to culture, one approach to healing would be to adjust the diet to reflect a different culture—as in replacing the emphasis on western grains with eastern rice products. For some, a vegetarian diet is helpful, and for others a high emphasis on meat products is required. If natives are subject to heath difficulties, they must change their diet to one more compatible with their own evolutionary path—which may differ markedly from the general beliefs about healthy eating.

When Chiron is intercepted the need to adjust our lifestyle by instinct or intuition may go critical. We may not rely on the experience of others around us. We may not live by their rules or according to their instruction. We must choose our own way in every aspect of life, trusting our inner guidance and relying on past-life experience and intuitive information.

The Effect on Virgo and the Sixth House

It is my opinion that Chiron has superseded Mercury as the ruler of Virgo. Consequently, its interception will affect Virgo and sixth house areas of your chart. Mercury

---

[1] A computer term, meaning that the work you have done is stored in memory for later retrieval.

clearly rules the brain and perception, but its rulership of the hands is less clear. However, the very name Chiron suggests *handling* and *hands-on*.

As ruler of Virgo, Chiron becomes the polarity point for Neptune, ruler of Pisces. If Neptune is the unconscious–or more accurately the sub- and super-conscious—mind, Chiron is the conscious mind. Intercepting Chiron will hide the way that our conscious mind works, usually because it is adept at using less-conscious mental resources.

Lacking conscious choice, the Virgo area of the chart may do a lot of wheel spinning. We may overanalyze and over-criticize possible choices. In the end our choices may seem more attuned to the *lesser evil* than to the *greater good*. Sometimes we seem to have lost the connection between cause and effect, so that we have difficulty learning from experience. This leads to a generally pessimistic attitude toward life. Because an intercepted planet is powerful, the result is that we create the very thing we feared. Worriers all, these people's worries are highly creative.

Worry

Do not try to stop worrying in traditional ways. Do not scold or criticize yourself.

Acknowledge that worry is an abuse symptom. Be gentle. Learn to laugh at yourself. Say something like, "There I go again," and say it with a rueful chuckle.

Instead, whenever you notice that you are in worry-mode, distract yourself. Do something that will engage your mind elsewhere. Some people read romances or watch sit coms or soap operas on TV. Some use exercise. It does not matter what you use, so long as it makes your inner critic shut up.

No fair criticizing yourself for the time it takes to do this exercise!

With Chiron intercepted, the sixth house may be out of balance during your early adulthood. The placement tends toward obsessive-compulsive behavior, and the body either gets ignored and abused or it gets so much attention that imagined injuries and ills become real. On the job, the attempt to do all things perfectly may make you so slow that superiors lose patience with you. Alternatively, you may be so ungrounded and spacey that you cannot be trusted to do your assigned tasks. (If this happens, you are in the wrong job. Use whatever form of prayer is comfortable, to ask for your right-work.)

Only making Chiron and the interaction between right and left brain conscious can entirely resolve the problem. For some this is a difficult placement socially because may interfere with normal maturation. Some natives seem unable or unwilling to grow up. The real problem is that their natural way of doing things is by applying mystical knowledge to mundane affairs. Since this is a largely unknown human ability, these natives must in time remember it for themselves. Until they do, their maturation is *stalled*. Remembering may involve research into a culture different from the one they incarnated into. Or, as is true of all interceptions, a significant move (east or west to a different time zone) can smooth the way to awakening previously unconscious areas.

The Appearance

The most obvious challenge of intercepted Chiron is getting past certain levels of development, or certain life experiences. In the less evolved, emotional development may progress to a particular level, and then arrest. Some retain the grandiosity of infancy, even while they learn to speak and function at a level that permits them to survive. Sometimes there is a fine ability to memorize roles, facts, ideas, and/or beliefs, with very little comprehension of meaning.

The slightly more advanced reach a higher level of maturity, such as emotional adolescence. This is a kind of *no man's land* between childhood and adulthood, where one is never certain whether those around us will expect dependence or independence. Many learn to hesitate and observe what others are doing before taking any action. These become reactors, more than actors, with little capacity for self-motivation. They wait to be told what to do, then, like adolescents, chose to rebel or comply. For them there is no *middle ground*, no individual choice available.

The interesting thing is that this lack of self-motivation often permits natives to *sit still*, to *be quiet*, to wait. In this space Neptune can float dreams, visions, and symbolic images. In this space intuition naturally develops to a higher than *normal* level. All that remains is for natives to begin trusting it. When they can *let go* all the forbidding parental voices, all the *shoulds* and *should-not's*, the garbled sound of clairaudience, or the blurred images of clairvoyance will clear up, providing excellent guidance. Gradually the habit of hesitation can be converted to checking with the internal information system, rather than the external environment. With practice, the process becomes faster and more automatic. In time the hesitation will be so slight as to become invisible. Natives will then reach their potential as conscious channels—those who speak from their internal information base as naturally as other speak from recent learning and experience.

The Reality

These are natural gurus. They become living examples of new methods for a new age. They are practical mystics and masters of reality. They are life's *efficiency experts*, who know how to take what is and adjust it for better function. Their faith is demonstrated by their works,[1] proving its practicality. In today's world, faith is a much scarred term. A clearer modern term for it is trust. Quite literally, Intercepted Chiron works through Nep-

---

[1] From the Bible, James 2 17-20.

tune, in a demonstration of the power available when we trust—life, ourselves, our Source.

In more modern terms it is about *effortless work*, about service without strain. It is about living a lifestyle, *not made with hands,* by affirmation, ritual, and visualization. It is intentional creation of form or information by forces or abilities that are invisible to the ordinary human senses. It includes trust in the *extra* senses, and the use of *paranormal* abilities for ordinary purposes—to get jobs, to heal, to produce necessities and luxuries, etc.

Only allowing oneself to be *hung up* on what seems unfinished or unexplained can prevent the manifestation of these abilities. It is, then, extremely important to let go the past. You must be willing to let your higher power deal with such issues, trusting it to handle what you cannot resolve. Doing this, your life has no limits, and you discover your true level of mastery.

These are they who need not learn, or practice, or observe, to know. Their knowing has evolved to a place in their being, so that they show up as *instinctive* or *automatic* magicians. Their lives are a living demonstration of the practicality of *trusting in a higher power*, however that power is perceived and by whatever name it is called. Ultimately, it is their task to heal the splits between *lower mind* and *higher mind*, between right-brain and left-brain, so that Mercury can make full use of the resources of a consciousness greater than we have ever before acknowledged. To this end, the secret hidden by the interception of Chiron is that these are *Servants of the Most High God/dess.*

Intercepted Neptune

Intercepted Neptune buries the possibility of living an unlimited lifestyle based on an essential trust in life under layers of experiential learning. This can look like a *loss of faith* or an inability to trust the benevolence and/or rationality of life. Faith is *unexplained knowledge*, something absorbed into identity so that it no longer has or needs words. We have no name for our faith, and we cannot explain it in ways that allow us to understand it. It is a *given* in every conscious act of our lives.

Neptune represents our capacity for trust in life. Trust is the quality that permits us to question, to draw inferences, and ultimately, to *live by faith*. The churches who have had so much to say about it have rarely named it correctly. Science comes closer when it speaks of *instincts*. When we depend on instincts, we live entirely by faith from its original meaning. We simply do what it is natural for us to do, trusting the rationality and benevolence of LIFE, assuming that our *instincts* will not betray us. In so doing, we live by the *unquestioned belief* that we know what we are doing. That is, and must be, a matter of faith, because the rationality of our actions can only be determined *after the fact*. The only criterion is "did it work?" The only valid judgement of that must be based on whether we learned something. If we learned anything, even that this method does not work, or that we need more practice, we have not failed.

The difficulty of this interception is that, going unnamed, our faith is relatively unconscious. Because we have no formal religion or philosophy of life, we do not recognize the deep and vital reality of our faith. Living from an undefined self-trust, our lives work best when our attention is elsewhere, and we seem to live by *blind luck* or *blind justice*.

The Dynamics of Intercepted Neptune

Intercepted Neptune puts it beyond our grasp. Neptune is the most difficult of all the planetary principles to grasp. Like smoke or water, it slips through our *fingers* whenever we try to hold and examine it. Think of it as a point on or segment of a circle. The circle has no end, and getting a sense of Neptune requires us to think of a circle as having an end. An old symbol, the Oureborus comes closest to presenting a visual symbol for Neptune. In it the rising *Kundalini snake* swallows its tail, forming a circle. Having done so, a spiral is implied. Every time consciousness crosses Neptune's field, it changes levels.[1]

Neptune is our capacity for masterful use of consciousness, but intercepted Neptune does not understand the principles of consciousness. Consequently natives are unaware of the possibility of mastery. These do not even consider the possibility of having more than five senses. Their definition of *faith* is *religion*. If religion fails them, they experience it as a loss of faith. Meanwhile, they live lives full of grief over the loss, never noticing that they have abilities and talents which function at the level of mastery. A friend once told this writer that he had no faith. She pointed out his outstanding mathematical skills, reminding him that every time he used them, it came from a place of trusting that the principles would always work. He was, in fact, living a great part of his life by faith—if only in the fact that mathematics would work for him and he could use it to solve problems. It is just such awareness that natives will be forced to notice. Until they do, their lives may be filled with examples of what and whom cannot be trusted.

Neptune is always present, even when we are blinded to it by an interception. To grasp Neptune at all, requires some understanding of the principles of evolution, especially as applied to consciousness. Every incarnation begins with a period that we think of as relatively unconscious. Initially, we have only our basic instincts, our inherent *animalistic* knowledge. Only when we learn language, do we begin to have a recognizable personal consciousness. We accumulate a data base of words, and learn simple file handling under Gemini and Virgo. The Jupiter function develops around puberty, adding the ability to infer reasons, concepts, and principles from the Mercury data. Gradually these abilities expand, until they lose spatial definition.

Meanwhile, the process *speeds up*, losing visibility, even as the blades of a fan disappear when their motion increases. Like the fan blades, intuition and instinct are simply logical calculations occurring at a speed that our perceptions cannot follow. When knowledge processes at that speed, it is *part of our identity*. We call it instinct, talent, intuition, or native abilities. These are thought processes so well mastered that we no longer need to focus our attention on them. Even as we learn to walk without attention or effort, so also, we learn to *think* without effort or attention.

---

[1] The old esoteric term is *vibration*. A newer one is *spin*.

Without a sense of the evolutionary principles, we cannot fully grasp Neptune's possibilities. We learned every instinctive action during some developmental period. When it is completely mastered, it moves into the realm of *unconscious*; we no longer need to focus attention on it. When the entire species has mastered some bit of learning, it becomes integrated into the species definition and is implied in the name of it. To say that humanity is a *thinking mammal* implies that it originated from an *unthinking one*, suggesting that at some point in time the species itself was incapable of real thinking. It is presently quite clear that humanity will soon require a new definition as an *intuitive being*. When the human species has intuition as a recognized characteristic, an entire new level of awareness will become possible. The definition of any life form is the baseline from which it evolves, rising in consciousness. Neptune symbolizes our capacity to master succeeding levels of consciousness.

Another Neptunian aspect is the impersonal or all-human mind, that *pool* of information that Intuitives can tap. Instinctives and those who *live by faith*[1] automatically rely on it.

Living by faith is the simple recognition that there are logical reasons behind all that we are, all that we do. It is a simple trust in life that allows us to function without questioning how we can do what we do, trusting that we were *made* perfectly and that we *know what we are doing*, whether or not we can explain it in words. This entire realm of information lies in the wordless domain, because it is yet unnamed, or because the name has become unnecessary or irrelevant. We need name only those things that we focus on. The automatic, instinctive, functions will perform without our attention and do not require naming. Instead, we must rely upon and trust upon them.

When Neptune is intercepted, this ability to perform automatic information processing is an unknown, unrecognized ability because it has gone unnamed or has been improperly named. The great difficulty it has struggled against during the Piscean age, was the attempt to moralize and rationalize it into nonexistence. It went so deep underground that the world's prophets, alchemists, and mystics were required to *go underground*. The most powerful Neptunes hid in interceptions, where they could perform best when they were ignored, and/or when the conscious mind was asleep or focused elsewhere.

Understanding its Effects

With an intercepted Neptune, recognition of the difference between faith and religion is a life imperative. Since your early environment defined faith in religious terms, you of-

---

[1]This is why we regard the sign placement of Neptune as a key factor in assessing the current *general* level of consciousness. As Neptune moves through the signs of higher evolution, the generations born come in with a higher *baseline* than the previous ones. This does not exclude individual evolution, which is keyed to the evolution of Mercury and Jupiter. Chiron probably refers to the *averaging out*, or synthesis of the three planets. Literally placed between Jupiter and Saturn, it also says something about our ability to cross our ego limits.

ten think that you have no faith. If you really did not, your life would not work because a workable lifestyle requires us to trust many unprovable theories. Wherever your trust is, there your faith is. Wherever your faith is, your life will work without attention.

Problems arise only when we question our perceptions of the results. Most misperceptions result from questioning our faith. When we say that we have no faith, we negate some portion of the belief in our capacity to make life work for us. If we are convinced that abstaining from church attendance or from praying in a prescribed way is a sin and punishable, it will be our own subconscious that will mete out the punishment. We will be punished as much as we believe we deserve.

Alternatively, the more we trust our *inner guide* to lead us in the appropriate directions, the smoother our journey becomes. In the Neptune realm, questioning the value of our natural instincts disrupts the creative flow. The only permissible questions are those such as, "Given that I have the necessary ability or resources to do this, what is the next step?" Most simply stated, Neptune's realm is the place where nature and God merge.

A popular cliche is: "What you see is what you get." Neptune reminds us that, "What you *look for* is what you get." Let those who doubt notice how quickly newly discovered diseases become epidemic in this age of media hype. We suggest that a major improvement in the quality of life would be achieved by simply reversing the balance between stories and advertising designed to fight death and those which affirm life. Neptune has long been given rulership of drugs. The significance of that may be greater than we have noticed. The *cure* has become a major *cause* of illness—especially when it has a high profit margin. It is easy to forget that advertising has an avowed goal of creating markets for its products.

We have long regarded Neptune, like Uranus and Pluto, as somewhat generational. In essence these planets are impersonal. Applied personally, they detail our capacity to recognize and use impersonal abilities in a personal way. Uranus allows individuals to *break out of* the consensus definition of humanity. When sufficient individuals have done so, Neptune will begin dissolving that definition. The first step in doing so can feel like being *nowhere,* lost in a *fog,* or *swimming in uncharted seas.* It takes considerable trust in ourselves or in some power that we may call on to venture into that place which has been called the void. The reasons we do so are based on logic.

When we have surveyed our lives and observed that certain abilities or circumstances have consistently worked for us, we can reasonably predict that they will continue to do so. However, consciously venturing into new realms of activity, based on that conclusion, can be frightening. Add too much fear to the equation and confusion is generated. We notice that we are *in a canoe without a paddle*, forgetting that we have already experienced the current and carefully calculated where it will take us.

The form that intercepted Neptune takes is that of *forgetting* the entire subject of faith, or at least of religion. Here we design our lives outside the context of religious practice, using forgetfulness to invalidate programmed guilt. Doing this, our lives will work at a particular level with minimal interference, but growth will be slow. The achievement of greater levels of freedom will be slow, steady, and plodding. Progress will be achieved, and a structure of security can be built, but slowly, brick by brick, sans magic or miracle. Here the principle of cause and effect operates in a strictly material fashion. Natives trust it without looking for another version of it in which invisible causes produce visible effects.

At random intervals, their buried faith in LIFE brings occasional unsolicited gifts and *coincidences* that keep them out of certain kinds of places and events. Rarely, if ever, do these beings get caught in destructive weather events. Even if they were present just prior to these events, they will be gone by the time they occur. Their investments will be equally protected, and members of their families seem to have angelic protection. Still, until the interception opens, natives seldom notice and almost never realize that the real *protection* that they have is their faith. Because they assume that life will work for them, it does. When they begin to worry about whether it will work for them, it gets shaky. Let them get busy and forget to worry, and life gets good again. Often this leads to the conclusion that rewards are the result of hard work. A clearer truth would be to say that hard work gets their personal consciousness out of the way of their ability to trust and have faith in the rationality and benevolence of life.

What they have the opportunity to learn is that *playing hard* will work as well, perhaps better, because the joy generated would power creation, producing even faster results. With Neptune intercepted, we must learn to trust our protection and our supply. As we do so, greater and greater realms of awareness will open for us. This is the mark of new possibilities and rising consciousness. It is the point where new versions of *psychic*/creative abilities develop. Intercepted Neptune predicts the possibility of conscious mastery, including the ability to work magic and miracles. It is probably the most difficult of all intercepted planets to retrieve, because it violates the known scientific laws. Functioning entirely in the invisible realm, its effects are completely visible to all. Still, with our human mandate to *name* everything, to explain it in rational terms, to quantify and qualify it, we lose touch with the mystery and the magic of life. When we do, the entire world lives outside Neptune's domain, as though it were intercepted in the all-human chart.

Literally, intercepted Neptune is sleeping Neptune. Because it is, natives often seem to require more sleep than most of their peers. For them, sufficient sleep may be more important than sufficient food, water, or other physical requirements. Many will be attracted, at some point in life, to the study of dreams. Alternatively, they will take dreaming entirely for granted, giving no thought to dream content. They assume that it is a natural function, like any other, and ignore dreams entirely.

The Effect on Pisces and the Twelfth House

Without its Neptune rulership, Pisces is relegated to Jupiter. It then becomes *unquestioned belief* . . . or dogma. Specifically, it forces Pisces to manifest only as confusion and fear, the elements that blur our ability to develop our inner senses. Pisces may then be a place where other people's feelings constantly intrude and dreams turn to nightmares. Only when we realize that mastery is possible while living on earth, can we reclaim the ability to use our inner senses consciously.

Its effect on the twelfth house is to relegate the contents of the twelfth to an unconscious that is filled with *sins*, fears, and negative feelings that often *sneak out* as compulsions. Effectively, it represents the inability to remember our soul wounds and/or the fear of doing so. Until we make Neptune conscious, the twelfth house remains a fearful unknown that may haunt our lives. No haunting has more nuisance value than the haunting of Intercepted Neptune. It will keep us *jumping at shadows* until we go looking for a reason why. Only then will we learn to trust our own perceptions and guidance. Doing that, we master our confusion and fear. It is replaced by faith in ourselves, our God/des, or simply in a rational universe. It matters not, for the meaning blends and all is one.

The Appearance

If faith is present, but unnamed or undefined, its essence is unconscious, therefore unlearned. It must, then, have been absorbed from the mother, through the bonding process. This makes it an emotional issue, existing completely outside the realm of thought. This allows it to continue its work, beneath awareness. This can look like, and probably is the reality of angelic protection. It literally symbolizes *automatic faith,* faith as an aspect of being, or inborn talent.

With Neptune split from Mercury, faith is split from consensus reality. It must function outside the general consciousness—as we have taught. When Neptune is intercepted, this becomes abundantly clear, because the faith that works in the lives of natives does not relate to current religious definitions of it. They live by faith continuously, mistaking it for reason. Their senses may work through the physical eyes, ears, etc., but that is only appearance. They really have a much wider perceptual range than is *normal* in their generation. Because it has been there from birth, they have not noticed anything unusual about it. Most do not understand that *everyone* cannot see, hear, understand, learn, as easily and quickly as they do. They take their exceptionally high intelligence for granted, sometimes downgrading it because it did not always conform to the lower perceptual standards of traditional educational structures.

What allows them to *dodge* most traumatic crises is this ability to *see, hear,* or otherwise perceive signals that are imperceptible to the average person. These translate directly into action, which can be explained logically, keeping them out of harms way. One might suspect that they can see behind themselves and/or that they have X-ray vision, judging by the results. Still, because this has always been their personal reality, they usually do not notice that others perceive an entirely different world.

Occasionally *accidents* can occur, but these originate with psychic attack. Because of the automatic nature of their faith, they will suffer more pain and/or inconvenience from these than real damage. It is between improbable and impossible that the same person could attack them more than once. The unconscious nature of defenses might allow an occasional breach, but the automatic responses would prevent another one from the same source.

Intercepted Neptune makes Pluto unconscious as well, but this is unimportant. Neptune is the *mystical master* while Pluto is the *alchemical magician.* As is currently shown by the literal passage of Pluto inside Neptune's orbit, his abilities are included within Neptune's *Ph.D. course*, so are irrelevant for intercepted Neptune.[1]

The Reality

While almost everyone else needs to make their faith conscious, learning to use the creative aspects of consciousness with intent, intercepted Neptune is the true master of life who has already moved beyond that point. These individuals need to notice, appreciate, and trust their own methods. For them, the proper uses of affirmations, visualizations, rituals or other forms of prayer is twofold. It is good to verbally recognize that their lives are already in the *hands* of a consciousness so highly evolved[2] that it needs no further attention or instructions.

The Master Jesus once said, "Take no thought for your lives, what you shall eat or wear, or where you will live." He instructed his disciples[3] to live like the sparrows and the lilies, fully dependant on the Divine Source for all their needs. These instructions are especially directed to intercepted Neptune natives. The less attention they give to the acquisition of *things* the more of these *things* will appear in their lives, sometimes quite miraculously or magically. Each would do well to affirm this until they entirely believe it.

The second and best prayer of all is the prayer of thanksgiving. Notice, value, and take delight in everything that appears in your life. Pay attention to and enjoy the blessings and opportunities attracted to you. Becoming more aware of faith's demonstrations, the more thankful you are, and the more goodness multiplies. Know that you have passed the level where need and desires are important. Gratitude for life's gifts is and must become

---

[1]This will probably not always be the case, since, in a few years, Pluto will return to its position outside Neptune's orbit. This suggests that new awareness will become available by then which will give Pluto even greater powers than he presently has.

[2]It does not matter whether you call it Self, God, Goddess, It, or whatever. It only wants to be greeted.

[3]These natives may well be reincarnations of the actual disciples.

a way of life. As it does, letting go of the hard work and learning to play gets easier. In the end, yours is the lesson implied in the command to *become as little children*. The more you trust your automatic supply and protection, the more you learn to live playfully, the better and more abundant your life will be.

Intercepted Nodes

To have an intercepted nodal axis can feel like having a major *short in our wiring*. Certain parts of our lives will be under-powered. Other parts will be overpowered. This can look like a *split personality*, but it is more like *split perceptions*. The effect is like having each eye see and/or each ear hear something different from the other. The double perceptions will periodically collide on the way to the brain and the circuits will become jammed.

The nodal axis represents the natural passage of energy, as focused attention, through our lives. We get attention at the North Node and give/release it at the South Node. The axis presents an image similar to that of a *float* that gauges the level of consciousness with which we enter life. In terms of consciousness, it is the polarity in which this axis resides that is significant. Which end rests in which sign and house tells us something about the ego program. In the *natural* progression of life, the two ends soon learn to cooperate sufficiently to lose individual definition.

When this axis is intercepted, no connection exists between attention given and attention received. More accurately, the entire concept of a need for attention goes unnoticed. It is assumed that, if the child survives, its needs are met, and no further attention is required.

The Dynamics of Intercepted Lunar Nodes

Because they form an axis, the dynamics of intercepted Nodes follow the patterns of intercepted signs, where polarities seem to exchange places. In each house, the sign composition of the interception presents a message about what you should/should-not be/have/do, and any planets add details. When the North Node is added, the instructions state that we should accomplish this without attention from others. In this area no one is going to show or teach you how to follow the instructions of the house. They take it for granted that you already know what is needed, so no one is going to *waste* their time and attention in teaching you. Because you must accomplish this learning task alone, it will take more of your attention than it would otherwise warrant. The effect is that of reversing the Nodes, so that instead of getting attention from others at the North Node, you are giving this house and sign all of your attention.

The sign of the North Node shows who gives us attention or when.[1] When it is intercepted, infants struggle for enough attention to stay in body, and children fight for sufficient attention to stay focused on learning. Sometimes natives get sick from lack of *feeding*—literally from lack of focused attention from an adult. If it takes people pleasing, being sick, or engaging in disruptive behavior to get attention, that is what they will do. Remember: Survival is the imperative and the *only* absolute morality.[2]

When we reach adulthood, the South Node should activate. It points to an area where we are expected to *pay attention*. The attention received from others at the North Node is intended to be passed on to others at the South Node. If we have not received sufficient attention from the adults in our childhood, we may mature physically, but will have certain aspects of our personality underdeveloped. This can be as debilitating as if one arm or one eye lagged behind in physical development. Usually we learn to adapt, but in some limited way. It is quite common for this type of physical disability to picture the psychological reality.

> Example: You can see, and you can even read, write, and learn with one eye, but you have no depth perception. Although you know that objects have depth, on occasion and in unusual circumstances, the inability to judge the location of objects in space can cause serious consequences. Seeing requires a disproportionate amount of attention/energy, because we cannot entirely trust our eyes.

The ego message of the South Node is "pay attention here." When intercepted, it reverses to "pay no attention here." The subliminal suggestion is that you should be able to do this with almost no concentration. Alternatively, it may suggest that this is not your *job* and that you should leave it to someone else. Getting the tasks of the South Node house accomplished is possible, but you are required to function from intuition and/or past-life memory. The things you know about this area of life may be well behind or ahead of the times. Because they are, they require more attention. Because you are programmed to *ignore* this area, the attention must come from another. In the house of the

---

[1] Examples: Sagittarius North Node gets attention from teachers. Cancer North Node gets/needs much nurture during early childhood, from Mother.

[2] This may account for the scarcity of examples in my files. It is probable that a large percentage of intercepted node natives do not survive or, if they do, may spend their lives in institutions.

intercepted South Node, you will probably feel the need for a mate, partner, or significant other who can give attention in this *forbidden zone*.

> Example: Intercepted South Node in the second may be emotionally programmed to *need* others to financially support him or her. This will conflict with the spiritual need to support the self. Investing all your money in the eighth house, so that it becomes *marital income* and not second house *personal income* can resolve this. Your partner takes charge of the money, and *gives you what you need*—out of your own money!

Keep in mind that this is the *Moon's* South Node. Ordinarily, this axis shows something that we learn from the family environment. When they are intercepted, the family environment does not contain the opportunity to do so. By default, any conditioning attached to intercepted nodes must be absorbed through the mother-child bond. The ego message they give is actually hers, and not ours. Some method of disowning the program by affirmation, visualization, ritual, or other form of prayer can be useful in releasing the nodal axis from interception. The release will then allow it to revert to its original position, removing the negatives. Then the North Node will receive attention/energy and the South Node will pass it on. Here we share what we are/have/or can do. Because we cannot teach/give without getting attention from the student/receiver, the axis begins to *spin*. This is the correct spiritual alignment for a fully empowered rise in consciousness, with the accompanying activation of Fortuna.

The Effects

An intercepted nodal axis causes it to reverse direction in the ego program while remaining in its original position in the spiritual identity. This amounts to instructions to teach what we have not learned and to learn what our spirit intended to teach. It causes serious snarls in our consciousness. Its effect is like putting plugs on both ends of an extension cord and plugging both into live outlets. Circuits for the entire house would probably be blown.

Human consciousness is more adaptable than electrical wiring, so the effect may not be so drastic; but it will certainly cause energy disruptions in body and soul. These disruptions will short out the passage of energy from Spirit to body to life. Literally it disrupts the connections between the Sun and the rising sign and house.

Solar energy is malleable and fluid, directed only by spiritual intention. That intention directs our choice of *wavelength*, or birth sign. This is the enlivening force, imaged in human reproduction by the sperm. The Moon then provides the directing principle for producing a form capable of following that intention on earth. The physical ovum symbolizes it. When the two connect, the solar identity joins the lunar purpose to produce a physical person from spirit and soul. While infants remain *hidden* within the womb, they are *fed* directly from spirit through the umbilical cord. Each fetus is alive, and has a type of preconsciousness, but full humanity is not conferred until it moves *out of the darkness* and *into the light* at birth. The *final act* in producing a human version of our spiritual intention is that of becoming visible to *our own kind.*

When the umbilical cord is severed, we can no longer draw sustenance directly from Source—in any conscious way. The paradox lies here. At the point of birth we begin to need attention, care, and feeding, from others. It is this nurturing process that makes us fully human. We continue to share feelings and feeling responses with our mother for months after birth. During that time our senses gradually develop and we learn to respond to them, essentially from her responses to them. While we are in a preverbal state, all communication is at the feeling level. The only person who can respond to us is the one who is sufficiently familiar with us to *feel our feelings*, to interpret and respond to them. While we may instinctively cry from discomfort, or coo from pleasure, we cannot really communicate before the development of language.

Sometime near the beginning of the second year (usually) we begin to develop speech. If we have other adults besides Mother to talk with, we will begin to separate *instinctual behavior* and learned behavior. We learn to express our feelings more precisely. Instead of a wail that means we are hungry, we can ask for a cookie. We consciously learn how to get the attention we need and this allows us to begin exploring our world, extending our horizons, expanding our awareness.

Literally, intercepted Nodes point to an interruption in this process at its beginning. Remember that all things lunar are connected to the beginning, or foundation, of life. The newborn child needs a great deal of attention. It needs to be fed and kept warm and clean. Still, a greater need sometimes goes unrecognized. For some time after it leaves the womb, the child needs considerable physical contact with the mother—or with some *warm body*. Without that it can feel abandoned, rejected, unvalued, resulting in a sense of loss, displacement, or dysfunction. With verbalization, those needs can sometimes be met, but the initial lack of attention to certain needs functions like an irreplaceable loss in our emotional foundation. Such a loss continues through life like a *gaping hole* in our psyche. It demands attention from someone.

When we reach adulthood, this becomes debilitating. By this time, we are expected to be self-sufficient, self-generating. Still, the *empty place* in our psyche, constantly *aches*. If we are to attend to adult matters, we *need* someone who will focus on this emotional need, someone who will provide the necessary human contact. If the need is great enough, it will feel like a survival imperative, as though we might die without this other person. Only one condition entirely fulfills us and makes us feel whole. It is that state we call *falling in love*. During this euphoric time, we are the complete focus of the other. We get our needs for attention completely fulfilled and we are completely satisfied and happy. We feel whole and healed.

Traditionally, falling in love leads to marriage. At some point, marriage usually leads to the birth of one or more children. After we marry, without a sustained effort, the romance generally begins to fade. Our partner has other interests and does not always give us all the attention we crave. Husbands get involved in careers. Still, a seductive wife can usually get the attention she craves, *if she has not been programmed not to do so*. Occasionally she has a child to get attention, but discovers that once the child is born, it gets the attention and she is *left in the cold*.

Male natives may function reasonably well, because most get some *feeding* at work. However, they want their woman at home waiting for them with plenty of attention. If she gets involved in a career or other interests, he will feel cheated and may become angry—just to get attention. The real problems come with the birth of children. Giving a man with intercepted nodes sufficient attention for his general well-being is nearly impossible for any woman caring for an infant. Additional children, increase the problem. If she also uses lack of attention to control him, if she expresses anger by ignoring him, his survival instincts will escalate his internal fear of abandonment to rage.

Since his anger seems irrational to himself and everyone else, it is important that he realize that it is coming directly from his survival instincts. Being ignored or going unnoticed is a critical situation for an infant. If the infant was required to survive on such minimal attention as to be constantly *on the edge* of losing form, fear pervades his/her emotional foundations. She or he is so emotionally needy that keeping him/her happy is nearly impossible for any length of time. She or he is, quite literally, terrified of going unseen because it feels like dying.

Physical responses to this neediness can take a variety of forms. Fluctuating energy levels are common and severe cases produce manic depression. Overweight is common because the body is trying to prevent starvation. Back pain presents a graphic picture of the *energy snarl*. Literally the spinal cord is the physical expression of the nodal axis. The energy flow pictured has been called Kundalini. When spinal misalignment disrupts it, we are presented with a picture of the energy problem that pervades our lives. *The umbilical cord and the silver cord picture its soul corollary*.

The Appearance

It may be years before natives are truly connected to their spiritual imperative. For them, staying *in body* always seems questionable. They can never entirely take life for granted because survival issues keep surfacing. The constant need for attention can create addictions to ego activity and confine their lives to its ego limits. When they try to reach for the spiritual meaning and intention of their lives, ego programming translates into a conscious mode. It creates any crises needed to stay focused into their learned tasks.

During the formative period, the notion of physical form as an expression of an invisible, spiritual energy, was unknown. Behind all these difficulties is a split between physical consciousness and spiritual consciousness. It suggests that there is a gulf between humanity and divinity than cannot be crossed, so the ideas that divinity could feed humanity or that humanity could feed divinity, have no place in the emotional structure.

Through the initial emotional bond[1] comes a feeling of abandonment by God. Because of it, we must depend on others or on ourselves. At the time when this is programmed we do not know the difference. It can *feel like* we have abandoned ourselves or been abandoned by God. This makes the need for others who see us, who love and care for us, critical. Without them we may die.

Sometimes the problem continues during childhood. Children must depend on adults for their needs. If our parents are not emotionally dependable, if too much of their focus is on their own survival, we live in fear at a time when we know that we are too young to fend for ourselves. Our *survival instincts* are all that we can fully depend on, so they control our attention, keeping us so focused on staying alive that we cannot begin to think about other things. We cannot develop sufficient trust in life for our emotions to mature properly.[2] We remain somewhat infantile, producing a condition often called grandiosity. Grandiosity is healthy in an infant. It is unhealthy in an adult, and sometimes dangerous in a parent.

Most of these natives would make excellent single parents. However, since natives are emotionally dependent, they feel a need to be married. They will then *marry a parent* and the instinctive reaction to having a mate is to require all their attention. A mate who is distracted, or one who ignores you, can leave you so emotionally drained that the needs of any children present can feel life threatening. We are conditioned to react emotionally, as though they were a threat to our lives. Meanwhile, the reality is that our rage has nothing to do with the children. It is the result of living in a relationship that does not—probably cannot—fulfill our emotional needs.

Becoming an adult means becoming responsible for meeting our own emotional needs. It means we can function with our *umbilical cord* severed because we recognize—however subliminally—the existence of the *silver cord*. When that awareness is subject to overwhelming survival fears, the need to keep the emotional connection with nurture uncut goes critical.

From this we can see that upon occasion, this placement would suggest a prenatal threat. It is literally a serious threat of losing our mother at so early an age that it becomes a significant part of our emotional structure. When it does, the real problem is that emo-

---

[1]Or occasionally through later sexual abuse or brainwashing.
[2]Most of the examples we could find were in Cancer-Capricorn. This pair of intercepted signs often shows arrested emotional development.

tions periodically overwhelm reason, making us dysfunctional. Since this is an axis, it always has a relational context.[1]

What is unconscious/forgotten, hidden from view by the interception, is that cutting a physical symbol does not mean that the spiritual aspect which it represents is also cut. The *new* science of Karelian photography takes pictures of auras. It has revealed that the aura, or energy field, of a missing physical part remains. This shows that although the umbilical cord is cut, the silver cord remains, keeping our physical structure connected to its spiritual source. Although we believe that we are keeping ourselves alive by following our ego instructions, the truth is that we have been divinely energized from the beginning. Had we not been, we would have died shortly after birth because we did not have sufficient attention during that period for survival.

When the Nodes are intercepted, the *silver cord* is buried under layers of conditioned fears. Our birth and early childhood experiences have so frightened us that we cannot get past our fears. Focusing clearly enough to see intangibles is impossible when the tangibles constantly threaten us. We lose sight of our spiritual connection and all our attention goes to preservation of the ego.

With the identity disconnected from the self-image, it must survive on/from the attention of those around it. Following the ego mandate is the only way we know to get the kind of attention that everyone else takes for granted. We try to please everyone, follow all the rules, comply with every known request, so that we will get the energy, approval, love that we need for survival. Often we become obsessive-compulsive from the need to perform perfectly and win the applause we need. Most of us are rather compulsive about pairing, but we can function alone quite well, if we allow ourselves to do so.

The Reality

The reality is that we do not really need all this attention because we are powered from outside ordinary reality. The problem that we have is that our emotions so cloud our senses that we cannot see our connection with Source. Although we *feel* starved for energy/attention, we cannot see how very little we are actually getting because we have no *files* in our personal consciousness to compare with.

The problem did not originate from lack of care or nurture. It is rooted in the inconsistency of that care and nurture. At times our caretaker becomes so focused on her[2] own

---

[1] Because any axis has one end in the personal half of the chart and one in the impersonal half. In addition, one end is in the conscious/visible half and the other is in the unconscious/invisible half. Until the axis unites, each end will function in an adversarial relationship to the other. It will have a clearly visible component, and a deeply invisible component. These will also be equal, so that as much of the problem is invisible as visible. Half of it is always out of sight.

[2] This is not limited to the feminine gender, but does refer to the primary caretaker who is usually female, usually our mother.

survival, that the psychic connection, which was our lifeline, was severed. We could only be sure of care or attention, when she was physically focused on us. Because of this, we did not learn to recognize *subliminal attention*. If those around us are not showing their interest in us, we cannot see it. If they are not looking at us, listening to us, touching us, we think that they have forgotten us and we experience a completely irrational panic. Since that seems crazy, we convert it to anger or grief and project it on someone who might be the *cause* of our emotional responses.

For most, this is so deeply imbedded that it is better to avoid the nuclear family relationship. We can be comfortably married, if, we can sustain romance. We also make acceptable single parents, if we have plenty of opportunity for social interactions, especially conversation with other adults. Children cannot give the attention or validation required by any adult, but since we do not expect them to, they do not trigger our survival issues. Since intercepted Node natives have a higher-than-normal need for this, it is important that they remain aware of the fact and plan their lives to provide it.

Occasionally, these individuals make good nuns and monks because they can focus on establishing a relationship with their *unseen partner*. Even so, they do much better in community, where social interaction is available. They need to be seen and touched. Without it, they will simply fade out of existence. It is extremely important that they take responsibility for providing these needs for themselves because it is unlikely they will ever be sufficiently *solid and visible* to attract and hold the attention of a significant other for a long period. If they are to function in the ordinary world, most will need a variety of romantic partners. They need to accept this as a good thing and refuse judgment. Being *in love* is exceptionally good for these natives and is the only time they can function at optimum levels of creativity. If they intend a life of high creativity, in one way or another that need for romance[1] must be met. If that means a living *soap opera*, so be it. There is no sin in it. Romance without love is impossible, and love is always and forever valuable.

Those who come into this world with intercepted Nodes take on the most difficult task of all. Required to live at the level of *pure instinct*, we must ignore all the rationalities that most of the world insists on. This can bring condemnation from self of others. Neither permit nor accept it. It does not belong to you. You can neither abandon spirit, nor be abandoned by it. Although your connection to earth and its consensus reality is tenuous, you have a correspondingly strong bond to your Divine or Cosmic Source. *Angels* constantly attend you. They will continue to surround you while you choose to remain visible on earth.

You, more than most, have the right to leave this world at choice. When you have finished what you came to do—and you will know it—simply move your attention away

---

[1] This is often mistaken for a sexual addiction because these are generally connected in our mind. This is far more about being seen and valued than it is about touching and sex.

from Earth. Immediately angel wings will lift you up and you will return to your real home, your real family. More than most of the Possibility People, you are *not of this world*. This is why it has never *fed* nor *satisfied* you well. The hunger you feel is for your real home, somewhere in another time, space, or dimension. You came as a volunteer, to spread love. Create as much love through romance, as much joy through beauty, as you can. After that, let go without guilt.

We have said that intercepted Pluto natives lead butterfly lives, living the transformation symbol. Intercepted Node natives go one step beyond. They enter this world as butterflies, plant the seed of the next generation of consciousness, creativity, or even children, then move on. Often not here for long, are they are not designed for physical labor or attention to laws and details. They come to add a little beauty to our lives and to show us that beauty is its own reason for being.

Intercepted Fortuna[1]

Intercepted Fortuna feels like our *luck* and/or our joy has been stolen. The adults in our childhood have taught us that we must earn whatever we want because luck is illusion. This takes much of the joy from our lives and we often lose our capacity to risk. Until the interception opens, the best we can hope for is a bland version of peace and contentment.

For a deeper understanding of what this placement means, try a different word. Let us rename it the Part of Delight. Examine the word DE-LIGHT. It means, *of the light*, and is a benefit of enlightenment. Fortuna most aptly describes a point in the chart where *lucky coincidence* gives us something that delights us. It is a point of desire fulfillment, where life brings us something *just for the fun of it*, and not because we are aware of wanting or needing it[2].

In the *normal* path of unfoldment, in order to discover the true capacity in our Fortuna, we must first have our nodal axis active. This means that we must have linked the attention received at the North Node to attention given at the South Node[3] so that consciousness/energy flows smoothly through our life. The nodal axis establishes an energy flow like electrical current. This in turn creates a magnetic field at the Part of Fortune which attracts good things to us. Fortuna events, are not so much *luck*, as they are *personal bonuses* or rewards for service at the South Node.

Ordinarily, Fortuna's rewards are *side-effects* of rising consciousness. DE-LIGHT! However, the emotional structure of Intercepted Fortuna is not *ordinary.* In our earlier

---

[1]Part of Fortune—drawn as a circle containing a cross or X.
[2]From the Bible, the measure is *pressed down and spilling over.*
[3]See *The Nodes of the Moon*, Rev. Alice Miller .

work on Fortuna, we stated that the transformation required to open interceptions normally starts with nodal activation. We can begin by energizing Fortuna, forcing activation of the nodal axis, but this shocks the system. Intercepted Fortuna is made conscious in exactly that way! The process is comparable to the old esoteric instructions for raising consciousness by energizing the chakras. It amounts to applying a severe (often literally electrical) shock to the system to *force it past* its ego boundaries.

The Dynamics of Intercepted Fortuna

Fortuna is a lunar Ascendant. The horizon in a geocentric chart describes the formal structure through which the Sun manifests. It is a solar Ascendant. If a human body is superimposed over such charts, the right hand will be at the Ascendant with the left at the Descendant.[1] Our natal Ascendant shows how we reach for life with the dominant hand, and the Descendant shows qualities that assist and support that reaching, similar to the function of the non-dominant hand.

Fortuna is an emotional Ascendant. It implies a Descendant, or Reflection Point in the opposite sign and house[2]. Personal benefits are described by Fortuna, and impersonal ones—or benefits to others are described by the Reflection Point. When the native is sufficiently self-realized to understand that whatever benefits me also benefits others, she or he can benefit from both ends of the axis. This then suggests *private* or inner enjoyment at the Reflection Point and *public* or visible/material benefits at Fortuna.

> Example: A writer with Fortuna in the ninth house can expect to attract publishers, but only after a rise in consciousness. A third house reflection point will show personal satisfaction or joy in the writing and readers will learn much from the works. This supports further publication.

As with the nodal axis, we can achieve a kind of spin. The difference is that the Nodes are more intellectual, while the Fortuna axis is more emotional. These are the two facets of consciousness. Together they define the "life and greater life" mentioned as Jesus's gift to the world. Nothing is more energy-producing than joy. The combination describes a system for energizing the entire being to increasing levels of awareness and creativity, predicting the accrual of *good fortune* and joy.

The Effects of Intercepted Fortuna

As we said, Fortuna describes a magnetic field. Imaging this as a magnet, we realize that all magnets have two poles, indicating a direction of flow in the magnetic force. We

---

[1] For this reason, we teach that charts of those born left handed should be turned $180°$ for reading.
[2] When you turn the chart for left dominance at birth, Fortuna must be refigured. The results will put Fortuna in the same house as the original unturned chart, but place it in the opposing sign. Example: With Fortuna originally in Capricorn in the tenth, turning the chart places Fortuna in Cancer in the tenth.

must properly align this to produce attraction. Reverse the alignment and our magnet will repel the same objects it would otherwise attract. Our *bonuses* or rewards for growing awareness will then be *shoved away* from us, discouraging the pursuit of expanding our awareness. Because of it, the price of pursuing enlightenment will be too high until we resolve our ego programming issues and open the interception.

As we learned in *Interceptions: Heralds of the New Age,*[1] any intercepted axis effectively reverses in our original programming. Because the house instructions include the signs at the beginning and ends of the involved houses, *but not the intercepted sign*, the rules of logic imply that the intercepted signs exchange places. When they do, the ends of the Fortuna magnet become misaligned with our personal energies, reversing the natural attraction to repulsion. The Part of Fortune then gives a very good demonstration as a Part of Misfortune.

Literally, we were conditioned to emotionally reject the things that would bring us our most delightful experiences. This is deep conditioning and part of the preverbal/emotional structure. We instinctively feel that these things are immoral, inappropriate, or not good for us. We may also feel that we have no right to them or insufficient strength of character or intelligence to handle them. Because our consciousness is creative, that conditioning creates our lives to *prove it*. However, interceptions *always* show that something extraordinary is present—hidden by the interception. Since the Nodes and Fortuna symbolize the energy system of rising consciousness, intercepting either of them hides the actual level of awareness, but it can never entirely de-activate it. *Miracles* happen spontaneously around such natives—whether noticed or not.

The Appearance

The underlying condition that *explains* us is that we enter a family where at least one parent has the capacity to *see* energy or sense our innate power. That person also functions under a general condemnation of human evolution. They are the type to assume that, if we became aware of the power, we would use it aggressively. They would be afraid of us and would react to us with fear and aggression. More accurately, such parents are afraid of the part of themselves reflected in their children, so they try to extinguish it. This possibility caused us to *bury it* in the interests of getting our survival needs met,[2] without causing our parents to incur more karmic debt.

Outwardly, *resistance* was infused into our consciousness through the bonding process. This compares to having an internal enemy trying to control our rising consciousness. This *enemy* has just enough power to attract punishment and lack where rewards

---

[1] *Interceptions: Heralds of a New Age,* Rev. Alice Miller, AFA.
[2] We suspect that investigation would reveal the kind of neglect that can cause a bright child to appear retarded.

and abundance were intended to come. The Part then becomes more Misfortune than Fortune, and our best efforts bring so little reward that long before adulthood we give up the effort of activating the nodes to raise consciousness. During this period, fulfilling our most basic needs requires all our conscious attention.

Eventually the interception opens and the polarity reverts to its original position re-aligning Fortuna with our being structure. Remember that transits of Uranus and Pluto are the primary activators of interceptions. If one of these conjuncts or opposes Fortuna there can be some dramatic events as Fortuna gets shocked into operation, forcing the nodal axis into activation and suddenly raising the vibratory level of the entire being.

When natives are sufficiently intent on spiritual growth to activate the nodal axis before the interception opens, they will encounter severe resistance from people bonded to them. Rising consciousness seems to attract *unlucky* events. More accurately, it leaves us vulnerable to ill will and psychic attacks because it is a magnetic/attractive area which has been turned in upon itself. It functions as a void which repels its natural fulfillment. It *looks like* a point of weak boundaries, as though it were a negative Saturn function, rather than a positive lunar one. Opposite Fortuna, we are undefended.

In our earlier work[1] we linked Fortuna to the Astral Body, noting that early in life it acts to collect and contain *negative* feelings and emotions. This makes it *dark* or *cloudy*. Since it normally surrounds the physical body, it provides an effective *smoke screen* behind which Possibility Person can hide their extraordinary abilities from those who would react negatively to them. As consciousness rises the nodal axis is activated and the astral body clears. Literally, our aura brightens, attracting attention from our enemies. Emotional vulnerability weakens our natural protective boundaries, leaving us open to psychic attack. We experience a rash of *coincidental bad luck* around the area of our intercepted Reflection Point. Such effects have been misinterpreted as Demonic attacks.

While these attacks are *evil*[2] *by nature*, their origin is very human. Very often they are directed by someone very close to us—usually a parent or mate—whose intention is to keep us under their control. Having eliminated this, secondary attacks powered by the negative area of the general consciousness can come from the area of our intercepted Fortuna. When that happens, hold fast to your faith, recognizing these as attacks on your goodness. The point of them is to load you with guilt, by making you assume that you deserve them. When that no longer works, they will cease, but it is a process, and does take time.

---

[1] *The Part of Fortune and the Astral Body*, Rev. Alice Miller.

[2] In the true sense. Evil is the antithesis of Life. The origin of such attacks is people whose attacks originate from the intention to stop the evolution of life. When evolution stops, life stops, resulting in the death of the human soul. In this case, the real target is the Earth and Physical Life. Perpetrators are trying to commit suicide by destroying their support system.

The Reality

Earlier we learned that an intercepted Moon referred to a mother who was emotionally shut down during the normal bonding period. We did not absorb the patterning needed for adequate emotional response to our physical feelings/needs. The Moon is the outer symbol for the principle by which energy is converted to matter and Fortuna is projected from it. Gradually we build a personal emotional structure, based on our bonding experience, and constructed from our experience of life. This structure will be *shaped* by our sense of security or insecurity in the world—by how much energy is required to stay in physical form. This *body of experience* shapes our *lunar Ascendant* or Fortuna.

With Fortuna intercepted, our experience often looks quite limited, as though we were *bonded to* some *species limits* that kept us from our mission in life. Very often, natives have almost no awareness of mission for a large portion of their lives. They might be very *ordinary* people, sometimes even a bit slow in unfolding. Often with little education or opportunity to expand their world, they drift through life—as though some part of their consciousness was in a coma.

When Fortuna is intercepted, the process of building an emotional body responsive to our needs occurs *in the background* of our life, remaining hidden until it gathers sufficient strength/power to survive the consensus reality into which it must be born. More graphically, our aura hides in the interception. When it does so, we often react to external causes that we intuitively sensed. Responding instinctively, we experience random *good luck* in the form of being *missed by* falling bricks and other *accidental* opportunities for injuries. Alternatively, we can be involved in events like auto wrecks without incurring injury. This shows that, even when unconscious, Fortuna has some protective power. However, when it must be entirely focused on protecting us from the ill will of powerful others, it does not always seem so *lucky*.

Because of the rising fear around human evolution,[1] intercepted Fortuna must hide its true nature and mission from the world until later in life. The structure of intercepted signs will offer a psychological explanation for this, but the reality is probably more a matter of timing. Readers will observe that intense shifting in the general consciousness began around 1988, and continues as we move through the twenty-first century. Many have called this period one of awakening. The significant factor is that the general population is becoming more aware and more accepting of phenomena based on a wider perceptual range. More people are seeing angels, extraterrestrials, nature spirits, etc. Their experience has begun to penetrate the general beliefs about the possibility of such experience.

However, the very *emotional nature* of intercepted Fortuna is sufficiently different from the general population to make the *energy radiation* of their emotions noticeable to

---

[1] James Redfield's *Tenth Insight* describes this.

many. It is as though the *color of their aura* is so different from the *norm* as to attract unwanted responses from those around them. It makes them *look like* a different species, but they are simply representatives from very advanced levels of human experience.[1] Whatever needs they have, are beyond our capacity to comprehend, and physical means cannot usually supply them.

Historically, humankind has had a habit of responding with fear and/or aggression to anything alien to our experience. Because this has happened during their *preparation period*, these natives must *hide their light*, keeping the astral body largely contained within the physical one. This is probably the phenomena behind cases where an otherwise *ordinary* person is suddenly enlightened through the auspices of some *accident*.

Psychic attacks often look like accidents, but these *accidents* have a *coincidental factor* about them. They happen when some series of events has caused us to be in *just the right place*, at *just the right time* to permit the accident to happen. With Fortuna intercepted, life is *turned around* when such an *accident* has a *fortunate* or *delightful* outcome. It is as though some attacker went *too far*, so that negative added to negative, creating a positive outcome.[2] We could also say that accumulated resistance suddenly converted to a catapult that caused us to bypass the period of delay, normally required to activate the nodes, as though it had never existed. We arrive at a point equal to or ahead of where we would have been without the delays.

We sometimes hear about these natives actually getting struck by lightening, or hit on the head, lapsing into a coma, and coming out of it with *new* abilities. The experience of an intercepted Fortuna resembles that of a walk-in but is actually different. Intercepted Fortuna, suddenly activated, drastically expands the awareness and abilities of its owner. The *new personality* is a result of this, not a cause.

In the final analysis we can state that intercepted Fortuna represents a more dramatic and obvious demonstration of the Possibility Mission than other interceptions do. These beings are absolutely *unknown quantities* for a large part of their life until some event *accidentally* reveals their true purpose. One day they have no awareness of their mission and the next it exists as a fully formed concept ready for application.

> Metaphor: Writing this, I am reminded of a movie. In it a wild young man, given to drinking and general *hell-raising*, experienced a severe accident, spent time in a coma, and *came back* with a great desire to do something with his life. He faced considerable resistance from family and friends who wanted the *original* person back. He struggled for some time, trying to find a niche for himself in a world that had seemingly changed *overnight.* We have no access to this man's chart, but strongly suspect that it has an intercepted Part of Fortune.

---

[1] These come from so far out in time or space as to be only vaguely describable here.
[2] Remember your mathematics: A minus plus a minus equals a plus.

Intercepted Fortuna represents a modern version of *angelic visitation*. Natives are probably *unconscious angels* hiding in human form. Each has a message for the world, but the message is one of such *shocking* proportions that a great drama is needed to surround it with validity in the current time-space.

Theirs is not an easy life, and contains little in the ordinary meaning of delight. Each is a living, breathing, miracle—only waiting to happen, at the right time, in the right place, to light up human experience. They lift us up, out of out darkness, into that great, shining, impersonal light that is God.

They have seen the *light at the end of the tunnel* and they have returned to reassure us that any tunnel we choose to follow, any path by which we seek, any method of evolution, will lead to the light. At the end of incarnation we always find the stars. At the end of human incarnational experience we become the stars!

This is the final interception, the final mission. Beyond it is a new kind of beingness, a new baptism of Spirit that fits us for yet another adventure. As so many are moving beyond the current definition of humanity, these are moving beyond the next one. They are, in fact, the *light at the end of the tunnel of human experience*. After that, who knows . . . . . Eternity beckons.

Finis

As we bring this book to a close, it ends with this question: "What is next?" The intercepted Fortuna attempts to answer that question, but its information remains vague and confused. At this point, we have reached the outer limits of the current capacity for understanding. To finally know the meaning of what we have attempted to present here, will be a matter of time—perhaps several or many centuries. For now our vision reaches no farther.

Let your mind play with what has been given. Among you, my beloved readers, I predict there will be one who will in time push the boundaries of our perception further. It is my hope and prayer that our work becomes a foundation on which other, younger people will build. Let us move forward together, continuing to build the future on the foundation of the past. This is the Light we seek. Out of yesterday comes today. Out of today comes tomorrow. The person who said that tomorrow never comes was wrong. Those who live today will create it. Go forth and do that, beloved readers. That is the greatest delight this writer can have!

Appendix I: House Polarities

Always interpret interceptions in terms of the full axis,
as first-seventh, second-eight, etc.

First House: The adults in your childhood say or imply that you are, or should be, like the sign on the cusps and any planets outside the interception, but not like the intercepted sign or any planets in it. As a result, your self-image seems to have a *hole* in it. You are in some way identified as one lacking in the intercepted area. It can be like having your hands tied or trying to study without sufficient light.

Seventh House: The adults in your childhood say or imply that you are not, or should not be like the sign on the cusps and any planets outside the interception, but your are or should be like the intercepted sign and any planets in it. (Because it is *not me*, it is projected on (usually significant) others. It is often part of the description of Mother because she is our first *other*.)

Second House: The adults in your childhood say or imply that you do, or should, have the sign on the cusps and any planets outside the interception, but not the intercepted sign or any planets in it.

Eighth House: The adults in your childhood say or imply that you do not, or should not, have the sign on the cusps and any planets outside the interception, but (instead) you should/do have the intercepted sign and any planets in it. (The eighth contains the childhood taboos that should/can be transformed into adult assets.)

Third House: The adults in your childhood say or imply that you do, can, or should, think/speak like the sign on the cusps and any planets outside the interception, but not like the intercepted sign or any planets in it.

Ninth House: The adults in your childhood say or imply that you do not, or should not, believe like the sign on the cusps and any planets outside the interception, but (instead) you should/do believe like the intercepted sign or any planets in it. (This is also instructions regarding what you should not think, speak, question, but only believe as you are told.)

Fourth House: The adults in your childhood say or imply that you do, or should, feel like the sign on the cusps and any planets outside the interception, but not like the intercepted sign or any planets in it.

Tenth House: While for the adult, the tenth is about public image, career and goals, for the developing child it has a different meaning. Here you are instructed that you do not, or should not, feel like the sign on the cusps and any planets outside the interception, but (instead) you should/do feel like the intercepted sign or any planets in it. Notice that unmet needs are great motivators and often become the stimuli for our goals.

Special Note: The fourth is *feelings*—meaning the basic ones: pleasure, pain, hunger, thirst, etc.—literally *mind of the body*, telling us what we need. Every feeling has a corresponding muscular response (feeling sad, we cry; scared, we run, etc.) These are e-motions, and reside in the tenth, so it becomes the ways in which we do or do not respond to our feelings and needs.

Fifth House: The adults in your childhood say or imply that you do, or should, act like the sign on the cusps and any planets outside the interception, but not like the intercepted sign or any planets in it.

Eleventh House: The adults in your childhood say or imply that we should or do react to the actions of others like the signs and planets outside the interception, but not like those inside it. It also describes the reaction of others to our fifth house activity. You may, however, initiate action according to the eleventh house interception, which will be reacted to according to the fifth house interception.

Special Note: Ultimately, the fifth is our role-in-the-family, and the eleventh is our impersonal role, or role in the world/universe.

Sixth House: The adults in your childhood say or imply that you do or should function like the sign on the cusps and any planets outside the interception, but not like the intercepted sign or any planets in it. While the outer shell of the sixth is about work/health, the intercepted part is about hobbies or play.

Twelfth House: The adults in your childhood say or imply that you are or should be *useless* according to the signs on the cusps and any planets outside the interception. This is because they are unconscious. When they act it is in a spontaneous, automatic way, as though being directed from some other realm. The adults instruct you to ignore them, forget them or take them for granted. Instead, you are instructed to use intercepted sign and planets, because they are conscious and can be used with intention. (As the sixth is about work/vocation, the twelfth is about play/avocation. So then *work on* the twelfth house interception and not the area outside it.)

Special Note: Instructions usually include the mandate to remember the outside part of the sixth, forgetting the interception, and forget the twelfth house, except what is intercepted—even if the house is on fire!!!! As a result, certain memories will be used to hide other memories. For example, the author recovered memories of incest, assuming them to be the cause of much difficulty, only to discover some years later than beneath the incest was infant battering by her mother. Only then did she realize the full power of her (intercepted Aries) survival instincts.

Appendix II: Current Planet Polarities[1]

To simplify, use the rulers of the sign polarities, as Libra-Aries is ruled by Venus-Mars. Cancer-Capricorn is ruled by Moon-Saturn. Otherwise, use the list below.

Three planets have double polarities. Generally, if Mercury lies in the signs Aries through Virgo, it will connect with Jupiter. If in the last six signs, it will connect to Neptune. If equal, it will begin life relating to whichever planet, Jupiter or Neptune, is placed lower in the chart, but can be shifted to the other. If in Sagittarius or higher, it will connect to both.

Venus follows the same rules with the planets Mars and Pluto. The rulership of Virgo is currently in transition. Many individuals with significant placements in Virgo are experiencing that at this time. Chiron is the vehicle of higher expression, and is lifting Virgo upward into a greater awareness of the inner senses, which are often experienced organically, as simply part of their structure—thus more instinctual than intuitive.

Mercury	Jupiter and/or Neptune
Venus	Mars and/or Pluto
Sun	Uranus
Moon	Saturn
Neptune	Chiron/Mercury

---

[1]These rules have been different in the past and will probably change in the future . . . possibly quite soon . . . within the lifetimes of some now living.

CPSIA information can be obtained at www.ICGtesting.com
Printed in the USA
BVOW030233100113

309877BV00005B/145/P